MIAMI
COCKTAILS

AN ELEGANT COLLECTION
OF OVER 100 RECIPES
INSPIRED BY THE MAGIC CITY

GABRIEL FERNANDO URRUTIA

CIDER MILL
PRESS

BOOK
PUBLISHERS
KENNEBUNKPORT, MAINE

13-Digit ISBN: 978-1-60433-826-3
10-Digit ISBN: 1-60433-826-1

This book may be ordered by mail from the publisher. Please include $5.99 for postage and handling. Please support your local bookseller first!

Books published by Cider Mill Press Book Publishers are available at special discounts for bulk purchases in the United States by corporations, institutions, and other organizations. For more information, please contact the publisher.

Cider Mill Press Book Publishers
"Where good books are ready for press"
PO Box 454
12 Spring Street
Kennebunkport, Maine 04046
Visit us online!
cidermillpress.com

Typography: Avenir, Copperplate, Phosphate, Rennie Mackintosh, Sackers, Warnock

Image Credits: Photograph of John Lermayer courtesy of Adam DelGiudice.

All recipe images photographed by Gabriel Fernando Urrutia, with the exception of pages 59 and 61, @cynlagos; pages 74 and 77, Coyo Taco; pages 88 and 91, Veza Sur Brewing Co.; page 122, DeepSleep Studio; pages 143 and 145, Kaido; pages 146 and 148, Food Comma Hospitality Group; pages 150, 152, and 154, Hakkasan at Fontainebleau Miami Beach; pages 157-158 and 160, Esotico; page 165, Anna Isabell Reyna; pages 171-172, KNR Hospitality; page 175, DeepSleep Studio; page 176, Anthony Nader; page 179, Liz Clayman; pages 180 and 183, The Miami Beach EDITION; page 185, Groot Hospitality; pages 193 and 195, Scarpetta by Scott Conan at Fontainebleau Miami Beach; pages 205-206, Stripsteak by Michael Mina at Fontainebleau Miami Beach; pages 209 and 211, Grove Bay Hospitality Group; page 216, Andrew Hektor; pages 262 and 265, EAST, Miami; page 266, Groot Hospitality; pages 268-269, Lost Boy Dry Goods; pages 275-276, Michael Pisarri; pages 283-284, Le Sirenuse at Four Seasons Hotel at the Surf Club.

All other images used under official license from Shutterstock.com.

Printed in China

1 2 3 4 5 6 7 8 9 0

First Edition

THIS BOOK IS DEDICATED TO JOHN LERMAYER.

HIS LEGACY WILL NEVER BE FORGOTTEN.

CONTENTS

INTRODUCTION

Miami has received many nicknames throughout the years, but the "Magic City" is the one that has stuck. Miami's rapid growth seems possible only through sorcery, and that growth is not limited to population and real estate; it refers to our vices as well. Miami was a haven for the Mafia during Prohibition, and a hub of the drug trade in the 1980s. This fast-paced expansion and growth, both good and bad, is at the heart of Miami. From its humble beginnings, Miami has grown into a world-class city, and its cocktail scene has grown right along with it.

Like any organism that undergoes a rapid evolution, the Magic City's path was cut by a few key moments. As the legendary Miami historian Dr. Paul George shares in his book, *Along the Miami River*, "[T]he mouth of the Miami River is one of the most important parts of southeast Florida history. Here is where, thousands of years ago, the Tequesta were settled, along with Jesuit missionaries among many others along the way. This was also the home to the 'Mother of Miami,' Julia Tuttle." Considered to be the only female founder of a major American city, Tuttle and her "magic" helped bring Henry M. Flagler's East Coast Railway to that same settlement in 1896. It was Flagler's railway that helped Miami flourish, transforming a town of less than 2,000 into the lively city we know today.

In the early 20th century, a devastating hurricane and the Great Depression threatened to sink this booming city. Ever resilient, Miami

remained afloat. The laws were not strictly enforced during Prohibition, which helped kick-start Miami's cocktail culture and its reputation for stimulating nightlife. Want a drink? Miami found a way. Need to head over to Havana? Less-than-legal flights were readily available, and Hollywood's favorite actors were itching to make their way down to Cuba. Like everything in Miami, the underworld grew like a weed during Prohibition, with everyone fighting for a piece of the pie. These notorious men and women braved rough seas and evaded law enforcement officers to make sure America's thirst for rum was quenched. These entrepreneurial folks, who became known as "Rum Runners," helped to keep Miami's spirits up during the Great Depression.

One of these rum-running gentlemen, E.W. "Red" Shannon, used his boat *Goose* to load up on liquor in Bimini for transport to Miami.

The Coast Guard were tipped off about his trip and were ready to seize the shipment. When Shannon heard about the Coast Guard he began dumping cases of liquor into Biscayne Bay to avoid being caught, but to no effect. Shannon met his end in a shootout with the Coast Guard at the grand Flamingo Hotel.

Another famous Rum Runner was Captain Bill McCoy. He sold his own liquor and focused on quality, something that often fell by the wayside during Prohibition. His dedication to providing the best for his customers earned his product the name "the real McCoy." While McCoy's operation wasn't based out of Florida, he did later retire there in a nod to Miami's bootlegging heritage.

South Florida even got in on the moonshine business during Prohibition. The shady Everglades were a perfect place to hide stills, and the dense vegetation made searching for a backwoods distiller all the more challenging.

These liquor loopholes routed successful businessmen through Miami. Thomas J. Peters, a hotelier, convinced a group of friends to develop a hotel on Bimini, where Prohibition was nonexistent. Just a quick plane ride away from Miami Beach, the Bimini Bay Rod and Gun Club was born in 1919. Soon, the Bahamas and Cuba became America's playgrounds, and everyone who came to play passed through Miami.

The 1960s brought a new wave of residents to Miami. As Fidel Castro's revolution took hold, Cubans began migrating to Miami in record numbers. This influx of Cuban culture, food, and drink changed the face of Miami forever. Amongst these new Miamians was the Bacardi family, who built the historic Bacardi building in 1963. Bacardi USA continues to operate out of Miami. Eventually, people of Colombian, Honduran, Haitian, and Peruvian descent also came in large numbers, which explains why cocktails like the Cuba Libre and the Pisco Sour became favorites in the Magic City.

Known as the "Gateway to the Americas," Miami has become a hot spot for Latin American culture in the United States. There are numerous locations in Miami where Spanish is the primary language, and in many parts of Miami it's possible to go without hearing any English whatsoever. This is part of what makes Miami so unique, as its blend of different cultures has created an incredible landscape for flavors and tastes to intermingle and inform one another.

Even though Miami has been a cultural melting pot for so long, cocktails were never at the forefront. While drinks like the Daiquiri and the Mojito became iconic here, a number of others have used Miami's lively and shadowy past to name their own concoctions (one cocktail, aptly named the Rum Runner, was invented in the Holiday Isle Tiki Bar in Islamorada during the 1950s). For a while, the Cosmopolitan, which the wonderful Cheryl Cook invented at South Beach's Strand in 1985, was the only Magic City creation that had made waves

on the global cocktail scene—and that was due in large part to the television show *Sex and the City*.

But in 2000, Dan Binkiewicz opened Purdy Lounge with the goal of bringing cocktails to the masses. His "no cover, no bullshit" stance was a far cry from the South Beach nightclubs that dominated the scene at the time, but Binkiewicz gained enough of a foothold to open people's eyes.

By the mid-2000s, the cocktail renaissance got ahold of the city and changed the way Miamians drink. In 2004, John Lermayer left New York and made his way to Florida to take a chance on the burgeoning Miami cocktail scene. Lermayer's move coincided with him becoming internationally recognized as a master mixologist. By focusing on fresh ingredients, classic cocktails, and hospitality at SkyBar at Shore Club, he pushed things to a level never before seen in Miami. In 2007, Lermayer was chosen by Lenny Kravitz and Ben Pundhole to open the Florida Room, which quickly became the center of craft cocktails in Miami. In 2010, the Florida Room was nominated for a prestigious Tales of the Cocktail Spirited Award for World's Best Hotel Bar, and became a springboard for famed bartenders like Gabe Orta, Richie Petronzi, Adam DelGiudice, Paul Sevigny, Angela Laino, Minas Kaliamouris, Lauren Andrews, Angelo Vieira, James Lagreca, Nick Bogado, Steven Hernandez, Rob Santiago, and Brian King. With Granville Adams hosting and Joshua Wagner working as general manager, Lermayer spared no expense in bringing the top educators and bartenders from around the world to champion spirit and cocktail education in Miami.

Clarke's in Miami Beach opened its doors in 2005 as a local neighborhood eatery and soon became a haven for bartenders and hospitality professionals throughout the United States. The owner, Laura Cullen, helped foster the city's cocktail movement by hosting drink-centric events at her establishment and by volunteering at Miami's United States Bartenders' Guild.

Soon after, Michelle Bernstein and her husband, David Martínez, opened Sra. Martinez in the Design District in late 2008. With help from award-winning bartender Julio Cabrera, who worked as their cocktail designer, their upstairs bar became an industry favorite and helped put Sra. Martinez on the country's cocktail map as one of *Esquire*'s "Best Bars" in 2011.

In 2009, Orta and Elad Zvi opened their company, Bar Lab, and provided consultation on menus for the opening of the W's Living Room in Miami Beach. By pushing progressive cocktails featuring fresh ingredients, the spot quickly became one of Miami's most popular craft cocktail bars.

As these important figures pushed Miami's tastes to the limit, talented bartenders began to emerge, and other bars sprouted up across Miami. In 2011, Haven Gastro Lounge opened with Isaac Grillo at the

helm, creating molecular, culinary-driven cocktails never before seen in Miami Beach. Blackbird Ordinary came in on Haven's coattails as a high-volume craft cocktail bar in Downtown Miami that featured a lively atmosphere, fresh ingredients, and a great spirits selection.

In 2012, Orta and Zvi transformed the cocktail scene yet again with the Broken Shaker, Miami's first cocktail pop-up that became permanent. Their attention to detail brought even more awards to Miami, as well as the honor of being listed (#14) as one of the World's 50 Best Bars in 2014. Their pop-up also earned the title of Best Hotel Bar at the Tales of the Cocktail Spirited Awards in 2015.

One year after the Broken Shaker stirred things up, the man who started the city's meteoric rise decided to turn traditional. Lermayer teamed up with old pal Wagner to create Miami's first classic cocktail bar, The Regent Cocktail Club. Here, Lermayer paired perfectly with Cabrera, Angelo Vieira, and Danny Valdez, creating one of the most dynamic bar teams in the United States. The Regent Cocktail Club is still a go-to for classic cocktails in Miami Beach and has received nominations for American Bartender of the Year (John Lermayer), Best American Bar Team, and Best American Hotel Bar.

The following years saw an astonishing amount of growth. Bars were popping up all over the place, and the historic Ball & Chain was resurrected from the grave.

In 2016, Orta and Zvi opened the Anderson Bar in Miami, which quickly stood out on the crowded scene and became a favorite of cocktail lovers. That same year, Lermayer partnered with Binkiewicz and Martínez to create the award-winning Sweet Liberty, which quickly became one of the best bars in Miami and the United States. In less than a year, Sweet Liberty won Best New American Bar, and landed at No. 27 on the World's 50 Best Bars. For the first time in history, Miami held two spots on the World's 50 Best Bars.

Unfortunately, John Lermayer's legendary run came to an end when he passed away in 2018. His loss was felt in cocktail communities around the world. On June 21, a memorial was held at the Botanical Gardens in Miami Beach, where hundreds gathered to celebrate his life. The City of Miami Beach Commissioners declared June 21 John Lermayer Day to celebrate his contributions to the Magic City. At this year's Tales of the Cocktail Spirited Awards, Lermayer was honored with the Helen David Lifetime Achievement Award for his notable contributions to the cocktail world. Sweet Liberty was awarded World's Best Spirits Selection and Best American Bar Team, yet another nod to Miami's stunning cocktail revolution.

Thanks to all these factors, and countless individuals, you can now find fresh, inventive cocktails all over Miami. There seems to be a cocktail competition or tasting every other week, and bartenders and hospitality professionals continue to pursue education to honor and further what Miami's cocktail pioneers built. Although some have left us too soon, their spirit will always be part of what Miami drinks.

FURTHER READING:

George, Paul S. *Along the Miami River*. Arcadia Publishing, 2013.

Ling, Sally J. *Run the Rum In: South Florida during Prohibition*. History Press, 2007.

Rum War at Sea. Treasury Department, United States Coast Guard, 1964.

HOW TO DRINK LIKE A MIAMIAN

- It's hot out there; don't be afraid of ice.

- Leave your long sleeves at home, and don't be afraid to wear that shirt with the tropical print.

- Shorts are allowed.

- 6:00 p.m. really means 6:30 p.m. (maybe later).

- Feel free to order in Spanish or English—or both.

- Treat your bartenders as you would treat a family member; this isn't a nightclub.

- Learn how to play dominos. There is nothing like a Cuba Libre and a good game with friends.

- Our hellos may involve a hug and a kiss on the cheek. Don't be shy!

- We live where you vacation, and we're always happy to host guests.

- You don't always have to order a Mojito, so don't be afraid to ask for a cocktail menu.

MIAMI-STYLE TWISTS
ON THE CLASSICS

In Miami, the Old Fashioned takes on different forms; try substituting rum for the whiskey for a Caribbean take on this classic drink.

Daiquiris and Mojitos are crowd-pleasers in the warm Miami sun. Go to your local farmers market for fresh, in-season fruit to elevate the experience. You can also try a shaken Daiquiri instead of a frozen one for a refreshing change of pace.

WHERE TO FIND INGREDIENTS AROUND THE CITY

Miami's melting pot of cultures and never-ending growing season provide a plethora of different fruits and exotic ingredients to use in cocktails. Miami has never been a place where you can open a bitters shop or specialty bar shop, as there is not a strong demand for them. That being said, local ingredients are easy to come by. Here are some of our favorite spots:

PALACIO DE LOS JUGOS (MULTIPLE LOCATIONS)

Not only can you get an authentic Cuban meal here, their fruits are sourced locally (and beyond) and are juiced and sold at low prices. Mango, passion fruit, guava, and guanabana juices are always on the menu and sold by the cup to thirsty locals who are looking for a cold, fresh drink. Looking to host a party? Stop in for a half-gallon and use it for a batch of punch at your next party. They also sell whole fruit in-house.

COCONUT GROVE ORGANIC MARKET

This open-air farmers market is only open on Saturday and offers a variety of organic fruits, veggies, and raw vegan foods in one of Miami's oldest neighborhoods. While you're picking up local fruit to use in your next Mojito, sample the tasty treats which local artisans offer up.

LINCOLN ROAD FARMERS MARKET

Sundays are the time for fresh fruits, vegetables, and even local honey in the heart of Miami Beach. This market has a Latin flavor, featuring chefs baking empanadas and small, Latin-inspired bites alongside ripe produce.

Redland Market Village

Take a trip down south to the Redlands and you'll see over 20 acres of fresh fruit, vegetables, and every other fresh good you could hope for. Fishermen stop in to offer their latest catch; the perfect pairing for that Martini and ceviche. Swing by their outdoor flea market for some vintage glassware and you're all set to start mixing.

Lucky Oriental Mart

We love Asian-inspired cocktails, but the ingredients aren't always easy to find. Located in a mini mall, this award-winning mart offers prepared foods, produce, and spices. This market is a one-stop shop for those exotic ingredients not found at your local grocer.

Robert Is Here

A local favorite that is family owned and operated in the heart of Homestead, this market has been around since the late '50s and sources produce from all over. You can expect to find lychees, fruit butters, marinades, honeys, hot sauces, and everything in between. Come for the selection, and save room for the milkshakes and smoothies—they make some of the best in Miami!

JoJo Tea

Opened in 2011, JoJo knows their tea. This is great place to stop in, pick up some new knowledge, and enjoy some delicious tea along the way. Don't be afraid to use some of their blends in your cocktails, as they can really shake things up.

Per'La Specialty Roasters

There is nothing better than a perfectly made Espresso Martini. In 2015, two locals named Paul Massard and Chris Nolte decided that Miami needed a roaster of high-end coffee beans. Not only are they incredibly knowledgeable in their craft, they're also very approachable, and are more than happy to expand people's understanding of coffee production.

Big Cypress Distillery

Want something different out of your rum? Look no further than Big Cypress Distillery. Make sure to ask for the self-taught distiller Fernando Plata, as his knowledge on the subject is extraordinary. Rum can be purchased on-site, with some special releases available depending on the time of year.

Sunset Corners

Looking for a rare Amaro or bitters? Look no further than Sunset Corners, the locals' favorite since 1954, when it first opened as a small package store. Here, you can find a healthy wine selection with some of the rarest liqueurs and spirits in Miami. They also support local crafters.

Mixology Ice

This company is dedicated to making some of the clearest ice in the United States. Cuban-born Carlos Leal and his team pair artisanal techniques with state-of-the-art technology to create custom ice shapes and cuts for restaurants and bars all over Miami. Don't be afraid to stop in for your home bar, as their ice is second to none.

YOUR MIAMI HOME BAR

If you really want to wow your guests, a small investment in the right equipment and glassware for your home bar is essential. Having the right tools can bring beauty to a bar cart or serving tray, and they can also inspire your guests to ask questions about what you're using in your cocktails. You should put at least as much effort into your cocktails as you put into the food you prepare. Remember, guests will probably have one steak, but they'll have two or three cocktails.

TOOLS (AND WHERE TO GET THEM)

Japanese-style jigger (Cocktail Kingdom, Umami Mart)
Cocktail shaker (Cocktail Kingdom)
Bar spoon (Cocktail Kingdom)
Cocktail strainer (Umami Mart)
Fine-mesh strainer (Amazon)
Julep strainer (Umami Mart)
Muddler (Amazon)
Juicer (Amazon)

OXO peeler (Target)
Mixing glass (Cocktail Kingdom)
Corkscrew (Amazon)
Glassware (local thrift shop)
Paring knife (Amazon)
Pour spouts (Amazon)
Hamilton Beach Blender (Amazon)
Cocktail picks (Crate & Barrel)

SPIRITS

Vodka
Gin
Tequila
Rum
American whiskey
Irish whiskey
Japanese whisky

Scotch
Brandy
Mezcal
Pisco
Canadian whisky

Liqueurs

St-Germain

Chinola passion fruit liqueur

Disaronno Amaretto

St. George NOLA Coffee liqueur

Dry vermouth (refrigerate after opening)

Sweet vermouth (refrigerate after opening)

Triple sec

Bénédictine

Raspberry liqueur

Ginger liqueur

Luxardo (maraschino liqueur)

Extras

Angostura Bitters

Peychaud's Bitters

Bittercube bitters

Filthy Olives

Filthy Cherries

Ice tray with spherical molds

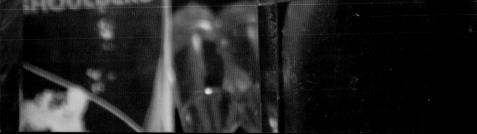

MIAMI

Locals can break down the city into countless official and unofficial neighborhoods. But all the featured establishments in this section can be found on streets that fall under the general umbrella of Miami.

— T#T —

AMARA AT PARAISO

Maria Pottage's riff on a Margarita blends tangy tamarind and bitter Campari for a sublime tequila cocktail.

GLASSWARE: Double rocks glass
GARNISH: Orange wheel

- 1½ oz. El Tesoro Reposado Tequila
- ½ oz. Campari
- ½ oz. agave syrup
- ½ oz. tamarind agua fresca
- ¾ oz. fresh lemon juice
- Orange zest salt, for the rim

1. Combine the cocktail ingredients in a cocktail shaker with ice and shake vigorously.

2. Strain over fresh ice into a glass half-rimmed with orange zest salt and garnish with an orange wheel.

FOR ORANGE ZEST SALT: Combine zest of 8 oranges with 2 cups kosher salt and mix thoroughly. Cover, label, and store.

FOR TAMARIND AGUA FRESCA: Start with tamarind base by roughly chopping 1 large piece of ginger and combining the ginger, 1 pound of tamarind pulp, and 1 mint sprig in a saucepan. Add 3 quarts of hot water to the saucepan and steep for 30 minutes. Strain through a chinois, label, date, and store in refrigerator. Take 10¾ cups of tamarind base and combine in large container with 8¾ cups cold, filtered water, 3¾ cups agave syrup, and 19 oz. lemon juice. Stir with bar spoon. Cover, label, date, and store in refrigerator.

— MONKEY BUSINESS —

AMARA AT PARAISO

The blend of bourbon and rum with banana makes this the perfect tropical sipper that packs a punch. At Amara, this cocktail is bottled and served ice-cold out of the freezer. No better way to beat the Miami heat!

GLASSWARE: Coupe
GARNISH: Dehydrated banana chip and toy hanging monkey

- 1 oz. Ron Zacapa Centenario Sistema Solera 23
- 1½ oz. Basil Hayden's Kentucky Straight Bourbon Whiskey
- ¾ oz. Giffard Banane Du Bresil
- 2 dashes of Angostura Bitters
- Dash of orange bitters
- 1½ oz. filtered water (only when bottling cocktail)

1. In a mixing glass filled with ice combine all ingredients and stir until cold.

2. Strain into a coupe and garnish with a dehydrated banana chip and a toy hanging monkey.

TO BOTTLE: Combine all ingredients in bottle, with no ice, stir until well mixed, and store.

— CLASSIC MOB MOVIE —

THE ANDERSON

Gabe Orta and Elad Zvi have built another fantastic team at The Anderson and this Godfather riff from Dave Simmons really stands out.

GLASSWARE: Martini glass

GARNISH: Orange expression and Filthy Cherries

- 2 oz. The Glenlivet Founder's Reserve
- ½ oz. Martini & Rossi Sweet Vermouth
- ½ oz. DeKuyper Amaretto
- 2 dashes of Angostura Bitters

1. Add all of the ingredients to a mixing glass filled with ice, stir until chilled, and strain into a chilled martini glass.

2. Garnish with orange expression and two cherries on a cocktail pick.

— MAI KINDA GAI —

THE ANDERSON

This is Miami's Mai Tai! Made with creamy cashew–banana orgeat, this is one boozy, citrusy, complex drink.

GLASSWARE: Rocks glass
GARNISH: Mint, orange slice, and a cherry

- 1½ oz. Hamilton 86 Demerara Rum
- ¾ oz. banana–cashew orgeat
- ½ oz. Mandarine Napoléon Liqueur
- 1 oz. fresh lime juice
- ½ oz. Ron Zacapa rum, to float

1. Combine all ingredients, except for the Ron Zacapa rum, in cocktail shaker with ice, shake vigorously, and strain over cubed ice into a rocks glass. Float Ron Zacapa carefully on top of the cocktail to create a layered effect.

2. Garnish with mint sprigs, an orange slice, and a cherry.

FOR BANANA–CASHEW ORGEAT: In a saucepan, bring 1 cup of cashew milk* to a simmer. Place 2 cups of granulated sugar in a container, pour the heated milk over it, and then stir until the sugar is dissolved. Let cool and then add 4 oz. of Giffard Banane Du Bresil liqueur. Stir until blended, label, and store.

Can be purchased, or made by soaking and refrigerating raw cashews in water overnight, blending the mixture, and then straining through cheesecloth.

— CANOE CLUB —

CASA FLORIDA

This cocktail brings out the delicate smoky notes of mezcal while staying tropical and fruity. A great drink for both mezcal lovers and those wanting to experiment more with the spirit.

GLASSWARE: Rocks glass

- 1½ oz. Ilegal Mezcal
- ½ oz. Crème de Mure
- ¾ oz. ginger–serrano syrup
- ½ oz. fresh lime juice
- 3 dashes of Peychaud's Bitters

1. Place all of the ingredients in a cocktail shaker, stir to combine, add ice, and then shake.

2. Pour over nugget ice into a rocks glass.

FOR GINGER–SERRANO SYRUP: In a saucepan, combine 2 parts sugar, 1 part water, 3 serrano peppers, and 2 large pieces of ginger. Cook until all sugar is dissolved. Keep cooking to taste and then strain out peppers and ginger.

— THE PINK FLAMINGO —

CASA FLORIDA

We are all suckers for a nice frozen cocktail. This riff on the Piña Colada combines floral flavors, tea, and coconut and ties them together with a Fernet-Branca reduction. Whoa!

GLASSWARE: Embassy glass

- 1½ oz. Banks 5 Island Rum
- ½ oz. pineapple-gum syrup*
- 1 oz. JoJo Tea Hibiscus
- ¼ oz. condensed milk
- ¼ oz. coconut cream
- Splash of Fernet–Branca reduction

1. Place all of the ingredients, except for the reduction, in a blender with ½ cup ice and blend until smooth.

2. Pour over the Fernet-Branca reduction into an embassy glass.

FOR FERNET–BRANCA REDUCTION: In a saucepan, combine equal parts Fernet–Branca and sugar and cook down until it has been reduced to a syrup.

This is a specialty product that locals pick up at Small Hand Foods.

— MONTEZUMA —

VISTA

This stunning cocktail offers the melon notes of Midori, the deep complexity of pisco, and the bright tang of kiwi and Sauvignon Blanc.

GLASSWARE: Coupette
GARNISH: Lime wheel

- 1 oz. pisco
- ½ oz. Midori Liqueur
- 1 oz. Boiron Kiwi Puree
- 1 oz. Sauvignon Blanc
- ¾ oz. simple syrup

1. Combine all ingredients in a cocktail shaker filled with ice and shake vigorously.

2. Double–strain into the coupette and garnish with a lime wheel.

FOR SIMPLE SYRUP: In a saucepan, combine equal parts water and sugar and heat until sugar is dissolved. Let stand until cool.

— MANIGORDO —

VISTA

A rum lover's dream! Three Plantation rums are tied together by tea and citrus notes in this tiki–style cocktail.

GLASSWARE: Tiki mug

GARNISH: Pineapple leaf, grated nutmeg, and a maraschino cherry

- ½ oz. Plantation 3 Stars Rum
- ½ oz. Plantation Pineapple Rum
- ½ oz. Plantation O.F.T.D
- ¾ oz. fresh lime juice
- ½ oz. chamomile syrup
- ½ oz. bergamot liqueur
- 3 dashes of Angostura Bitters
- 1 oz. pineapple juice

1. Combine all ingredients in a cocktail shaker filled with ice and shake vigorously.

2. Strain into the tiki mug and garnish with the pineapple leaf, grated nutmeg, and maraschino cherry.

FOR CHAMOMILE SYRUP: In a saucepan, bring 2 cups of water to a boil and then add 4 cups of sugar. Stir until sugar is dissolved, add 10 bags of chamomile tea, remove from heat, and let steep. When cooled down, strain syrup, label, and store.

CORAL

GABLES

Coral Gables is a city within Miami developed in the 1920s by the architect George Merrick. It is popular for being home to many acclaimed restaurants and bars while adhering to the strict building and zoning regulations that give this city filled with Mediterranean Revival architecture its stunning character.

— VOODOO CHILD —

THE LOCAL CRAFT FOOD + DRINK

This Michael Albuerne creation incorporates tiki and Taiwanese into one beautiful cocktail.

GLASSWARE: Pilsner glass
GARNISH: Mint sprig, seasonal flower,
cocktail umbrella, and a boba straw

- 2 tablespoons popping passion fruit boba*
- 1 oz. fresh lemon juice
- ½ oz. cashew–infused Falernum
- ½ oz. orgeat syrup

1. Place the popping passion fruit boba in the pilsner glass and set it aside.

2. Place the remaining ingredients in a cocktail shaker filled with ice and shake vigorously.

3. Fill the pilsner glass with ice and strain the cocktail into the glass. Garnish with a mint sprig, seasonal flower, cocktail umbrella, and boba straw.

FOR CASHEW–INFUSED FALERNUM: Lightly toast 1 cup cashews in a skillet until lightly browned. Pour 4 cups Falernum into a mason jar and add the toasted cashews. Let steep for 48 hours, strain the cashews out, and store.

Available at specialty stores and online.

— LOCAL TEA PARTY —

THE LOCAL CRAFT FOOD + DRINK

Barbara Peña Mehnert had Miami's incredible bounty of local ingredients in mind when she decided to use honey and lychee for this tropical tea cocktail that you'll want to drink all summer.

GLASSWARE: Vintage tea cup, with saucer

- 2 oz. The Botanist Gin
- ¾ oz. lychee–infused honey
- ¾ oz. fresh lemon juice
- ¼ oz. blackberry–infused Salers Aperitif
- 1 sprig of rosemary
- Spoonful of Chartreuse

1. Place the gin, infused honey, lemon juice, and infused Salers Aperitif in a cocktail shaker filled with ice. Shake until combined and set aside.

2. Place the rosemary sprig in the tea cup, add the spoonful of Chartreuse, and then ignite the Chartreuse.

3. Once flaming, double–strain the cocktail into the tea cup.

FOR LYCHEE-INFUSED HONEY: In a saucepan over low heat, cook down 1 quart of lychees with ½ quart local raw honey and ½ quart water for a half hour. Remove pan from heat and let stand for several hours. Strain, label, and store.

FOR BLACKBERRY-INFUSED SALERS APERITIF: Add 2 pints of blackberries to 1 bottle of Salers Aperitif and steep for a week. Strain, label, and store.

WYNWOOD

Miami's entertainment district, which is famous for its wall murals, has become a haven for great bars, restaurants, and breweries. There is not a day that goes by where you can't find an event or happening in Wynwood.

— LYCHEE DAIQUIRI —

There's nothing like a hand-shaken Daiquiri when you're in Miami. Add a bit of lychee syrup and it's a game changer. Enjoy this one with friends while sitting under the sun.

GLASSWARE: Coupe

GARNISH: Lime wheel

- **2 oz. white rum**
- **1 oz. fresh lime juice**
- **¾ oz. lychee syrup**
- **2 dashes of Bittercube Jamaican #2 Bitters**

1. Place all ingredients in a cocktail shaker filled with ice and shake until chilled.

2. Strain into a coupe.

3. Garnish with a lime wheel.

FOR LYCHEE SYRUP: Remove skin and seeds from 8 oz. of lychees and puree. Pour puree into a saucepan, add 1 cup sugar and 1 cup water, and cook over medium heat, while whisking, until desired consistency is reached. Remove from heat, let cool, label, and store.

— HAPPY ENDINGS —

1-800-LUCKY

Salty, smoky, and sweet, this surprisingly tropical cocktail has it all, and the cantaloupe-wasabi reduction ties everything together.

GLASSWARE: Highball or Collins glass
GARNISH: Lime wheel

- 1½ oz. El Jimador Tequila
- ½ oz. Ilegal Mezcal
- 1 oz. cantaloupe–wasabi reduction
- 1 oz. lime juice
- Dash of celery bitters

1. Place all of the ingredients in a cocktail shaker filled with ice and shake until chilled.

2. Strain into a highball glass.

3. Garnish with a lime wheel.

FOR CANTALOUPE–WASABI REDUCTION: Remove skin and seeds from a cantaloupe and puree. Pour puree into saucepan, add an equal amount of sugar, add wasabi powder (in small amounts to taste), and whisk over medium heat until desired syrup consistency is reached. Let cool, label, and store.

— FLOR DE JALISCO —

BAR ALTER

If you love a good tequila-and-mezcal cocktail, this one is for you. Gustavo Peña's creation strikes the perfect balance between sweet and smoky thanks to a jam made from in-season strawberries.

GLASSWARE: Clay cup
GARNISH: Pineapple leaves, lime wheel, and a marigold flower

- 1½ oz. Altos Olmeca Reposado Tequila
- ½ oz. Del Maguey Vida Mezcal
- ½ oz. strawberry jam
- ½ oz. agave syrup
- ½ oz. lime juice
- Dash of Black Lava Solution
- 3 dashes of Bittermens Hellfire Habanero Shrub

1. Place all of the ingredients in a cocktail shaker filled with ice, shake until chilled, and strain over ice into the clay cup.

2. Garnish with 2 pineapple leaves, a lime wheel, and a marigold flower.

FOR BLACK LAVA SOLUTION: Combine 2 parts water and 1 part Black Lava Salt in a saucepan. Bring to a boil, remove from heat, and whisk until the salt has dissolved.

— PILLOW TALK —

BAR ALTER

The botanicals in the gin play off the dandelion bitters in this floral cocktail, and the apple air elevates the drink.

GLASSWARE: Rocks glass or Irish coffee mug
GARNISH: Baby's breath blossoms and absinthe mist

- 2 oz. Martin Miller's Gin
- ½ oz. Gran Classico Bitter
- ½ oz. simple syrup (see page 43)
- ½ oz. fresh lemon Juice
- 3 dashes of dandelion burdock bitters
- Apple air, for topping

1. Place everything but the apple air in a cocktail shaker filled with ice, shake until chilled, and strain over ice into the glass.

2. Top with the apple air.

3. Garnish with a baby's breath blossoms and absinthe mist.

FOR APPLE AIR: Place 1¼ cups fresh apple juice, ¼ teaspoon citric acid, ¼ teaspoon salt, ½ teaspoon sugar, 1 teaspoon xanthan gum, and ½ oz. Versawhip in a bowl and whisk until well combined.

— ROSE COLORED GLASSES —

BEAKER & GRAY

This light, wine-based sipper from Ben Potts is a perfect way to get the evening started.

GLASSWARE: Highball or Collins glass
GARNISH: Rosemary sprig

- 4 oz. Rosé
- 1 oz. rosemary syrup
- ¼ oz. elderflower cordial
- ¼ oz. St–Germain

- 1 oz. fresh watermelon juice
- ¾ oz. lemon juice
- 1 oz. soda water

1. Place all ingredients, except for the soda water, in a cocktail shaker filled with ice, shake until cold, and strain into a glass filled with ice.

2. Add soda water and garnish with the rosemary sprig.

FOR ROSEMARY SYRUP: In a saucepan, bring 1 cup of water to a boil. Add 1 cup sugar and stir until clear. Remove from heat, add 1 tablespoon rosemary leaves, cover, and let stand for 36 hours. Strain and store.

BEAKE[R]

EATERY · BA[R]

MOVERS & SHAKERS:

After starting his career under the tutelage of Dan Binkiewicz at Purdy Lounge, Ben Potts opened Beaker & Gray and hasn't looked back. A native of Miami who wanted to provide great cocktails and food in an intimate yet casual setting, Potts runs Beaker & Gray with his best friend from childhood.

— THE HALLIWELL —

Ben Potts knows there is nothing like strawberries and mint in Miami's heat, which is why he put them in this refreshing vodka cocktail.

GLASSWARE: Highball or Collins glass

GARNISH: Mint sprig

- 1½ oz. Stoli Vodka
- ½ oz. Cocchi Rosa
- 1 oz. ginger syrup
- 1 oz. fresh lemon juice
- 1 oz. strawberry puree
- 8 mint leaves

1. Place all of the ingredients in a cocktail shaker filled with ice, shake until cold, and double–strain into a glass filled with ice.

2. Garnish with a mint sprig.

FOR GINGER SYRUP: In a saucepan, combine 2 cups simple syrup (see page 43) and ½ cup white sugar and simmer until the sugar is dissolved; then add 1 cup of ginger juice. Add more simple syrup if you want the syrup to be sweeter.

— LAVAGAVE —

BEAKER & GRAY

Ben Potts's blend of lavender-agave syrup and smoky mezcal makes for a good-looking and refreshingly tart cocktail.

GLASSWARE: Coupe

GARNISH: Grated lavender buds

- 1½ oz. Don Julio Blanco
- ½ oz. mezcal
- ¾ oz. lavender–agave syrup
- ½ oz. grapefruit juice
- ½ oz. lime juice
- ¾ oz. egg white
- Dash of Bittercube Cherry Bark Vanilla Bitters

1. Place the ingredients in a cocktail shaker filled with ice, shake until chilled, and strain. Remove the ice from the shaker, return the cocktail to the shaker, and shake it once more.

2. Pour the drink into a coupe and garnish with grated lavender buds.

FOR LAVENDER–AGAVE SYRUP: Place 1 teaspoon of lavender buds in a sachet. In a saucepan, bring 1 quart of agave to boil, remove from heat, add the lavender sachet, and let steep for 2 hours. Remove sachet and store the syrup.

DIVE BARS

High-end cocktail joints are wonderful things, but so are dive bars, and these are some of the city's best.

MAC'S CLUB DEUCE was not only Anthony Bourdain's favorite dive bar, it's also a favorite of the locals. This bar is open 7 days a week from 8:00 a.m. to 5:00 a.m.—including holidays. Opened as the Club Deuce in 1947, Mac's was founded in 1964 by Mac Klein, who lived to the ripe old age of 101.

CHURCHILL'S PUB is Miami's original punk club. Churchill's opened in 1979 and moved to its current location in 1980, where you can catch live music from hip-hop to hardcore and everything in between. Stop into Miami's best record store, Sweat Records, to pick up some vinyl on the way out.

DUFFY'S TAVERN on 57th Avenue has been a neighborhood favorite since 1937. The name has changed over the years, but the bar has not; it remains a well-known sports bar with great wings and a fun staff.

HAPPY'S STORK LOUNGE doubles as a liquor store and is well known by locals in North Bay Village. In the 1950s, well-known faces like Frank Sinatra could be seen taking a break from Miami Beach at the bar. Make sure to stop in for a beer and feel free to continue sipping while perusing the liquor store.

BRYSON'S IRISH PUB is a staple in Miami Springs. This beauty opened its doors in 1926 thanks to Glenn Curtiss, who was the founder of the aircraft industry in the U.S. A favorite of local airport crews, this bar sits near the Miami International Airport.

THE BAR is a Coral Gables favorite in the heart of Miami. Coral Gables was a dry city during its incorporation in 1925. In 1946, that all changed with the opening of The Bar on Giralda Avenue.

FREE SPIRITS is on 21st Street, right in the heart of Miami Beach. An industry hangout, this bar is open every day from 12:00 p.m. to 5:00 a.m.

ON THE ROCKS is another beloved neighborhood bar on the north side of Miami Beach. If you pop in, expect karaoke, inexpensive drinks, and great conversations.

CUCU'S NEST BAR is another great dive in Miami Beach. This one is housed under the Triton Tower condominium complex, so you should expect to bump into a lot of locals. Also expect karaoke and shots at odd hours. Doors open at 2:00 p.m. and close at 5:00 a.m.

SEVEN SEAS has been open for over 30 years, and the crowd of regulars has settled upon trivia and karaoke as pastimes. You can enjoy this beauty till 2:00 a.m. every day except for Sundays.

— BLACKER THE BERRY, — THE SWEETER THE JUICE

COYO TACO

With mezcal as the base, this beauty sings with picante and sugary notes. Enjoy this one with some of Coyo's world-famous tacos.

GLASSWARE: Highball glass
GARNISH: Lime wheel and sage leaves

- 5 blackberries
- 1½ oz. Montelobos Mezcal
- ¾ oz. St–Germain
- ½ oz. ginger syrup (see page 69)

- 2 dashes of Bittermens Habanero Hellfire Shrub
- ¾ oz. fresh lime juice
- ½ oz. agave syrup

1. Muddle 5 blackberries in a highball glass and add crushed ice.

2. Place the remainder of the ingredients in a cocktail shaker filled with ice, shake, and strain into the highball glass.

3. Garnish with a lime wheel and sage leaves.

— BRUJERIA —

COYO TACO

The marriage of tequila and the salted and spiced give this gorgeous cocktail a dynamic flavor profile.

GLASSWARE: Rocks glass

GARNISH: Strip of orange peel

- 1½ oz. Casamigos Reposado
- ½ oz. Union 55 Rum
- 2 dashes of Angostura Bitters
- ¼ oz. agave syrup
- Dash of activated charcoal*

1. Place all of the ingredients in a mixing glass filled with ice, stir until cold, and strain over a large cube of ice in a rocks glass.

2. Express orange peel over the cocktail and then use as a garnish.

Can be purchased online; in this recipe the dash is for color and nothing more.

— ROSEMARY'S BABY —

GRAMPS

Created for Gramps by the late musician and bartender Louis Salgar, the blend of Earl Grey, rosemary, and citrus tie this gin cocktail together. Unfortunately, Louis is gone. But this summery cocktail lives on at this legendary bar.

GLASSWARE: Rocks glass
GARNISH: Charred rosemary sprig

- 1½ oz. gin
- ¾ oz. rosemary–Earl Grey syrup

- ¾ oz. fresh lemon juice

1. Place all ingredients in a cocktail shaker filled with ice and shake until cold.

2. Strain over ice in a rocks glass.

3. Torch the rosemary until it is charred and then place it on top of the cocktail.

FOR ROSEMARY–EARL GREY SYRUP: Place equal parts sugar and water in a saucepan and cook over low heat until the sugar is dissolved. Add 8 bags of Earl Grey Tea and the leaves from 15 sprigs of rosemary. Remove the pan from heat and let steep for 20 to 30 minutes. Once cool, strain, label, and store.

IN MEMORIAM:

Louis Salgar was a local musician and bartender who was well loved by both communities. Louis's adventurous spirit allowed him to make the most of the creative space available in the cocktail world. He worked in legendary Miami bars such as Sra. Martinez, Broken Shaker, and Gramps, and his cocktail recipes live on at Gramps, as well as in this book. Salgar had a strong respect for the industry and often delved into the competitive side of bartending to show off his creative chops. His infectious laugh automatically made you feel at home at the bar, and his willingness to share the cocktails he was working on made you feel valued. In the wise words of Gramps, "Lives have been made more joyous, magical, musical, and savory because of you." Thanks to his enormous gifts, Louis's memory will long live in our community.

— GRAMPS OLD FASHIONED —

GRAMPS

If Miami had a signature Old Fashioned, it would be this one, which is made with rum instead of whiskey.

GLASSWARE: Rocks glass
GARNISH: Strip of orange peel

- 2 oz. añejo rum
- ¼ oz. black pepper syrup
- 2 dashes of Angostura Bitters
- 2 dashes of orange bitters

1. Combine all ingredients in a mixing glass filled with ice and stir until chilled.

2. Strain over ice into a rocks glass and garnish with a strip of orange peel.

FOR BLACK PEPPER SYRUP: In a saucepan, combine 1 cup demerara sugar, 1 cup water, and ½ oz. crushed black peppercorns. Cook over medium heat until sugar is dissolved. Remove from heat and let sit for 2 hours. Label, strain, and store.

MOVERS & SHAKERS:

A lawyer by trade, Adam Gersten transformed an unremarkable Wynwood property into Gramps, a now–legendary bar in the heart of the neighborhood. Adam spared no expense in filling the bar with relics from the '70s and '80s and building an incredible cocktail menu for a high–volume establishment. Come in anytime and enjoy a consistently delicious cocktail and consistently solid entertainment.

IN MEMORIAM:

Cameron Scholderer was a graduate of Florida International University's School of Hospitality and was a creative, hard-working bartender who loved to participate in cocktail competitions. He worked with the Morgans Hotel Group, Broken Shaker, W Hotels, Zuma, and KYU, which allowed him to cross paths with some of the best in the industry. His caring spirit and loving soul will not soon be forgotten.

— WYNWOOD MULE —

KYU

KYU in Wynwood is responsible for some of the city's artiest cocktails, and the addition of smoked pineapple makes this mule a masterpiece.

GLASSWARE: A repurposed can (which can be created by
cleaning a used can and removing the label);
or a copper mule mug
GARNISH: Pineapple leaf and a dehydrated lime wheel

- 1½ oz. vodka
- 1 oz. lime juice
- ¾ oz. smoked pineapple syrup
- 2 oz. ginger beer

1. Combine all ingredients in the can and add crushed ice.

2. Garnish with a pineapple leaf and dehydrated lime wheel.

FOR SMOKED PINEAPPLE SYRUP: Smoke 4 to 6 whole pineapples for 3 to 4 hours in a smoker until blackened. Allow to cool before chopping to retain the juices. Prepare water and sugar (60 percent and 40 percent, respectively, of total pineapple weight in grams). In a saucepan, combine chopped pineapple and water and bring to a rolling boil. Maintain for 15 minutes, then dissolve sugar into the mixture and simmer for an additional 45 minutes. Puree mixture, strain through a mesh chinois, label, and store. Alternate method: Slice pineapple and place slices on grill, cook for about 15 minutes, and then follow same method.

— TOM KYU GAI —

KYU

This is one of the more complex and unique cocktails at KYU. It is served warm and the blend of cilantro, chili oil, and the botanicals in the gin fuse for an exotic experience.

GLASSWARE: Porcelain bowl

- 1½ oz. Bombay Dry Gin
- ¼ oz. fresh lime juice
- 3 oz. soup batch
- 1 spoonful of cilantro foam
- 1 cilantro leaf
- 1 dehydrated lime slice
- 5 to 7 drops of chili oil

Place the gin, lime juice, and soup batch in the bowl and stir to combine. Top with the cilantro foam, cilantro leaf, dehydrated lime slice, and chili oil.

FOR SOUP BATCH: In a saucepan, combine 135 oz. unsweetened coconut milk, 15 cups coconut water, 2¾ cups galangal juice, 1¾ cups galanagal root debris (left from juicing, wrapped in cheesecloth), 1¼ cups thinly sliced lemongrass, 1¼ cups chicken broth, 1 tablespoon kosher salt, 1 tablespoon kaffir lime leaves, 2¾ cups scallion syrup and bring to a boil. Simmer for 1 hour, let cool, strain, label, and store.

FOR SCALLION SYRUP: In a saucepan, combine 4 cups water, 8 cups sugar, and ½ cup minced scallions and bring to a boil, stirring to dissolve sugar. Remove from heat and let scallions steep for 15 minutes. Strain, cool, label, and refrigerate.

FOR CILANTRO FOAM: Add 1 tablespoon sucrose esters to ¾ cup cilantro water and whisk with electric milk frother.

FOR CILANTRO WATER: Place 4 oz. cilantro and 5¼ cups water in a blender and puree until smooth. Strain, label, and store.

— VEZA SUR SHOOT THE MOON —

VEZA SUR

There is nothing like the flavor of guava during the summer in Miami, and the way it mingles with the Campari syrup and citrus ensures that this beer cocktail hits the spot.

GLASSWARE: Collins or highball glass

GARNISH: Mint leaf

- ¾ oz. Campari syrup
- ½ oz. fresh lemon juice
- ¼ oz. guava puree
- 8 mint leaves
- Veza Sur Guava Sour*

1. Combine all ingredients except for the Veza Sur Guava Sour in a glass.

2. Add ice and Veza Sur Guava Sour and stir to combine.

3. Garnish with a mint leaf.

FOR CAMPARI SYRUP: In a saucepan, combine 1 cup water and 1 cup sugar. Cook over medium heat, while stirring occasionally, until all sugar is dissolved. Bring to a boil and then reduce to a simmer for 5 minutes. Remove from heat and add 1 tablespoon Campari. Cool to room temperature, label, and store.

If you are unable to find this specific beer, use your favorite fruity sour.

— VEZA SUR SEASONAL MICHELADA—

VEZA SUR

When the summer heat is on high, who doesn't love the invigorating balance of citrus and saline in a well–made Michelada?

GLASSWARE: Pint glass

GARNISH: Lime wheel and a pickled bell pepper

- ½ oz. Búfalo Mexican Hot Sauce
- ½ oz. fresh lime juice
- ½ oz. pickled bell pepper juice
- Dash of Tajin
- Veza Sur Latin Lager*

1. Combine all ingredients except for the lager in a pint glass.

2. Add ice and top with lager.

3. Stir to combine and garnish with a lime wheel and a pickled bell pepper.

If you are unable to find this specific beer, use your favorite lager.

DADELAND

Dadeland is a small entertainment district made famous by the Dadeland Mall. Now this area, which borders Kendall, Glenvar Heights, and Pinecrest, features some of Miami's best restaurants and bars.

— EL PURO —

ABI MARIA

It only makes sense that this rum bar has devised this beauty of a cocktail.

GLASSWARE: Coupe

GARNISH: Torched cinnamon stick

- 2 oz. Zafra Rum
- ½ oz. cinnamon syrup
- 2 dashes of Angostura Orange Bitters
- 2 dashes of Bittercube Blackstrap Bitters

1. Combine all ingredients in a mixing glass filled with ice and stir until chilled.

2. Strain into a coupe and garnish with a torched cinnamon stick.

FOR CINNAMON SYRUP: Let 15 cinnamon sticks steep in 1 quart of simple syrup for 4 to 5 days.

— ONE DROP —

BARLEY AN AMERICAN BRASSERIE

This herbaceous cocktail marries citrus, basil, mint, elderflower, and the botanicals in this local gin for a striking easy sipper.

GLASSWARE: Wine glass
GARNISH: Lime wheel and a mint sprig

- 2 oz. Big Cypress Magic City Gin
- 1 oz. fresh lime juice
- 1 oz. simple syrup (see page 43)
- 1 oz. St–Germain
- 4 mint leaves
- 4 basil leaves
- 2 dashes of Bittermens Hopped Grapefruit Bitters

1. Combine all of the ingredients in a cocktail shaker filled with ice and shake vigorously.

2. Double-strain into a wine glass and garnish with a lime wheel and mint sprig.

— TABLE 32 —

Macerated berries and a homemade orgeat make for a refreshing drink that also allows the bourbon to shine.

GLASSWARE: Collins glass
GARNISH: Mint leaves and edible flowers

- 2 oz. Old Forester bourbon
- 2 oz. macerated berries
- 1 oz. fresh lime juice
- ½ oz. orgeat
- Soda water, to top

1. Combine all ingredients, except the soda water, in a cocktail shaker filled with ice and shake until chilled.

2. Strain over fresh ice into a Collins glass and garnish with mint leaves and edible flowers.

FOR MACERATED BERRIES: In a large bowl, combine 1 cup blueberries, 1 cup sliced strawberries, 1 cup raspberries, 3 tablespoons Old Forester bourbon, and 1 tablespoon sugar. Stir gently until all ingredients are mixed. Let sit for 7 days (or overnight if in a hurry). Strain, label, and store.

FOR ORGEAT: In a saucepan, combine ½ quart white sugar and 1 quart almond milk and cook over medium heat, while stirring constantly, until the sugar dissolves. When mixture is about to boil, remove from heat and cover. Let cool for a minimum of 2 hours, then add orange blossom water and almond extract. Label and store.

NORTH

MIAMI BEACH

orth Miami Beach, once known for its clothing-optional beach, has attracted popular chefs from all over and retained its art deco charm from the 1920s.

— DRUNKEN RABBIT —

TAQUIZA

Sipping from a pineapple will have anyone going tropical, especially if you are on the beach under the Miami sun!

GLASSWARE: Emptied pineapple
GARNISH: Pineapple leaves, orange slices, bouquet of mint, Tajin, and a cocktail umbrella

- 2 oz. Bosscal Mezcal
- 1 oz. Ancho Reyes
- 1½ oz. pineapple juice
- 1½ oz. guava juice
- 1 oz. cinnamon syrup (see page 97)

1. Combine all ingredients in a blender with one scoop of crushed ice and blend until smooth.

2. Pour the cocktail into the pineapple and garnish with pineapple leaves, 2 orange slices, a bouquet of mint, Tajin, and a cocktail umbrella.

— SHAKE YOUR TAMARIND —

TAQUIZA

This is another refreshing cocktail that perfectly pairs with Taquiza's award-winning tacos. The tamarind brings some tangy notes that highlight the blend of tequila and mezcal.

GLASSWARE: Clay cup

GARNISH: Mint leaves and a cinnamon stick

- 1½ oz. Tequila Avion Reposado
- ¼ Gracias a Dios Mezcal
- ¼ oz. Campari
- ¾ oz. tamarind concentrate
- ¾ oz. cinnamon syrup (see page 97)
- ¼ oz. fresh lime juice

1. Combine all of the ingredients in a mixing glass filled with ice and stir until chilled.

2. Double-strain into a clay cup and garnish with mint leaves and a cinnamon stick.

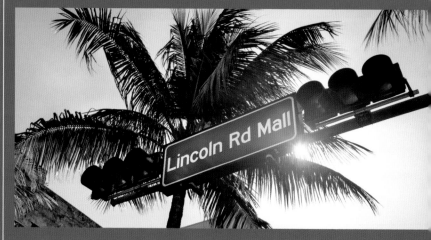

NOT-TO-BE-MISSED MIAMI

Miami is more than beaches and bars. So be sure to check out some of these destinations in between sunbathing and imbibing.

LINCOLN ROAD

This road is blocked off to cars and is for pedestrians only. Created in 1912, Lincoln Road houses farmers markets, restaurants, and retail shops. This is a must-see spot in Miami Beach and a great place to sit with a cocktail and people watch.

STILTSVILLE

This group of wood houses on stilts, which sits 1 mile south of Cape Florida on Biscayne Bay, is a gorgeous example of Miami's crazy past. The shacks were built in the '20s and '30s and were allegedly used for gambling. They have taken on many forms over the years, but today they are largely uninhabited and are used for photo shoots, special events, and weekend retreats.

OCEAN DRIVE
The iconic Ocean Drive is the face of Miami Beach. With its preserved art deco stylings and neon signs, it's no wonder that tourists flock to this area. Stop into Mango's Tropical Café for a Mojito and soak up the atmosphere.

FREEDOM TOWER
Originally the headquarters of Miami News, the tower became a symbol of freedom when the government used the vacated building to process immigrants coming from Cuba in the 1960s. Today, the building is owned by Miami Dade College, which uses it as a museum and educational center.

ALFRED I. DUPONT BUILDING
The Alfred I. duPont Building was built in 1939 and became a symbol of growth in Miami. Today, it is an event space that

has left many of the art deco finishes unchanged.

LITTLE HAITI
Historically known as Lemon City, this area of Miami became home to Haitian immigrants. Its cultural events are all influenced by the residents' French Creole background, and the food is always incredible.

COCONUT GROVE
The oldest neighborhood in Miami, dating back to 1825, Coconut Grove became known for its bohemian proclivities. This village by the bay boasts great restaurants, art galleries, and a walkable area full of parks and sidewalk cafés.

VIZCAYA MUSEUM AND GARDENS
The former villa of businessman James Deering, this historical landmark on Biscayne Bay highlights Italian Renaissance architecture. Built between 1914 and 1922, Vizcaya is now used for special events, tours, and film shoots.

BACARDI BUILDING

The former headquarters of Bacardi, the Bacardi Building is an art deco gem on Biscayne Boulevard in Miami. Designed in 1963, this iconic building is now the home to the National YoungArts Foundation, a non-profit organization.

THE FILLMORE MIAMI BEACH AT THE JACKIE GLEASON THEATER

In 1964, Jackie Gleason filmed his show in Miami Beach in this location. The theater was taken over by the Fillmore company and now hosts concerts for Miami's music lovers.

MIAMI MARINE STADIUM

Another historical landmark in Miami, this gem was built in 1963 to watch powerboat racing, as well as concerts and other water competitions. Since its close in 1990, it has become a hot spot for graffiti artists, who have turned it into a colorful attraction.

MIAMI BEACH

ncorporated in 1915, Miami Beach has taken on many forms throughout the years, from art deco capital of the world to celebrity haven. Now it serves as a destination for chefs and bartenders from all over the globe.

— PASS THE BOWL —

This is one of the most popular legacy cocktails at 27 Restaurant, which is considered one of the best restaurants in Miami Beach. It was created by Randy Perez, who wanted to create an Indian-inspired Margarita. The tantalizing result is tamarind, coconut, and agave curry served in a wooden bowl.

GLASSWARE: Wooden bowl

GARNISH: Lime wheel and a mint sprig

- 1½ oz. coconut fat–washed tequila
- 1 oz. fresh lime juice
- ¾ oz. tamarind shrub
- 3 dashes of curry bitters*

1. Combine all of the ingredients in a cocktail shaker filled with ice and shake vigorously.

2. Double-strain into the wooden bowl and garnish with a lime wheel and mint sprig.

Available online; to make your own, it would be most helpful to have an iSi cream charger and Dave Arnold's book Liquid Intelligence.

FOR COCONUT FAT–WASHED TEQUILA: Purchase coconut flakes and let them infuse with the tequila of your choice.

FOR TAMARIND SHRUB: Get a big container and acquire a pack of tamarind from any store (usually about ½ oz. or so per box). Peel off the skins from each tamarind piece and put peeled parts in large container. The ratio for any shrub is 3 parts sugar, 2 parts water, and 1 part vinegar. Add just the water and let sit for a few minutes. Once the meat of the fruit has been softened (with clean hands or gloves) start massaging the tamarind to release all the flavor. Once properly massaged, add sugar and vinegar. Stir until completely diluted, seal container, and let sit. The longer shrubs sit, the better they taste.

— BANGKOK, BANGKOK —

27 RESTAURANT

This was the first cocktail on the menu from Josh Labrada. Inspired by a restaurant that served Thai teas, this rye-and-tea infusion is created in a mid-16th century Japanese cold-brew coffee maker.

GLASSWARE: Collins or highball glass
GARNISH: Any available fresh herb

- 1½ oz. rye whiskey, infused with Thai tea and autumn spices*
- ¾ oz. Thai tea reduction
- ½ oz. Meletti Amaro
- 1½ oz. coconut cream
- 2 dashes of Bittermens Hopped Grapefruit Bitters
- Torched autumn spices, to top

1. Combine all of the ingredients in a cocktail shaker filled with ice and shake vigorously.

2. Strain into glass, top with torched spices, and garnish with herb of your preference.

FOR THAI TEA REDUCTION: In a saucepan, combine 3 parts sugar and 2 parts water. Add some Thai tea, bring to a simmer, and let the mixture simmer for 10 to 12 minutes. Let cool and then strain through cheesecloth.

*Labrada originally infused the whiskey using a mid-16th century Japanese cold-brew coffee maker. The rye and Meletti would be poured in the top container and left to slowly drip over local Thai tea, hazelnuts, autumn spices (cinnamon, nutmeg, clove, star anise, allspice, etc.), and cranberry hibiscus. A standard cold-brew coffee maker can also be used.

— SPRING IN TOKYO —

AZABU MIAMI BEACH

The Shochu in this recipe is made with local rice and lemongrass. When paired with yuzu juice and the bitter-plum flavor of the umeshu, it makes for a sublime drink.

GLASSWARE: Rocks glass

- ¾ oz. Mizu Lemongrass Shochu
- ¾ oz. umeshu
- ½ oz. yuzu juice
- ½ oz. simple syrup (see page 43)
- ½ oz. egg white

1. Combine all of the ingredients in a cocktail shaker filled with ice, shake until chilled, and strain.

2. Remove ice from shaker, return the cocktail to the shaker, and shake again.

3. Strain over an ice sphere in a rocks glass.

— EL VATO SWIZZLE —

BROKEN SHAKER

This Bar Lab creation is a gorgeous, modern classic at one of the world's best bars—the El Vato Swizzle elevates the Margarita with fresh watermelon juice and the homemade Mexican pepper reduction. Add a pinch of cilantro from Broken Shaker's garden, or yours, and there is magic in a glass.

GLASSWARE: Footed Pilsner glass
GARNISH: Watermelon slice and cilantro

- 1½ oz. Olmeca Altos Tequila Plata
- 1 oz. fresh lime juice
- ¾ oz. fresh watermelon juice
- ¾ oz. Mexican pepper reduction
- Dash of Peychaud's Bitters, to top
- Large pinch of fresh cilantro

1. Build all of the ingredients, except for the bitters, in a footed Pilsner glass.

2. Swizzle to combine, top with the bitters and crushed ice, and garnish with watermelon slice and cilantro.

FOR MEXICAN PEPPER REDUCTION (be sure to do this in a well-ventilated kitchen; the fumes from cooking the reduction will make the air extremely peppery): In a saucepan, combine 4½ quarts water, 10 dried chile de arbol peppers, 10 ancho chili peppers, 6 jalapeños (sliced lengthwise, 4 with seeds, 2 without), bring to a boil, and cook for 20 minutes. Strain into a mixing container. Due to evaporation during the boiling process, approximately half a quart of liquid will be lost (this has been accounted for in the ingredient quantities). Re-measure to ensure the end volume is 4 quarts of liquid. Add 6 quarts granulated sugar and stir continuously until sugar is completely dissolved. Let cool to room temperature. Label, date, and keep refrigerated.

— BITCH DON'T KILL MY VIBE —

BROKEN SHAKER

With herbs from the garden, this ideal summer vodka drink elegantly fuses basil and peach.

GLASSWARE: Collins glass
GARNISH: Pineapple slice and pineapple leaves

- 1½ oz. Absolut Elyx
- 1 oz. fresh lemon juice
- ¾ oz. garden basil reduction
- ½ oz. Giffard Crème de Pêche

1. Combine all ingredients in a cocktail shaker filled with ice and shake vigorously.

2. Strain over ice into a Collins glass and garnish with a pineapple slice and pineapple leaves.

FOR GARDEN BASIL REDUCTION: blanch ½ pound of basil leaves and then immediately shock them in ice water. In a blender, combine basil with 1 quart simple syrup (see page 43) and blend. Finely strain all the leaves out of the syrup and store in the refrigerator.

— COCOA PUFF OLD FASHIONED —

Cocoa Puff–infused bourbon reinvents the Old Fashioned. The chocolate and bourbon become best friends in this decadent yet balanced drink. Another modern classic from the folks at Bar Lab.

GLASSWARE: Rocks glass

GARNISH: Strip of orange peel

- 2 oz. Cocoa Puff–infused Old Forester bourbon
- 5 drops of white soy sauce
- 2 dashes of chocolate mole bitters
- ¼ oz. simple syrup

1. Combine all ingredients in a mixing glass filled with ice and stir.

2. Strain into a rocks glass containing a large ice cube and garnish with a strip of orange peel.

FOR COCOA PUFF–INFUSED OLD FORESTER BOURBON: Add one box of Cocoa Puffs to one bottle of Old Forester bourbon. Let sit for 1 day. Strain, label, and store.

MOVERS & SHAKERS:

Gabe Orta and Elad Zvi were intent on elevating hospitality in Miami, so they opened Bar Lab in 2009. In 2012, their lives changed forever with the opening of the legendary Broken Shaker at Miami Beach. Through education and their own tropical cocktails, Orta and Zvi helped transform the Miami cocktail scene, bringing it to a place where it could impress patrons from all around the world. The Broken Shaker has been named one of the World's 50 Best Bars for three consecutive years.

— THE PROJECT —

CIBO WINEBAR

Cibo Winebar is a staple in Miami Beach, bringing beautiful interior design and Italian food to South of Fifth. The Project slips rum into the space typically reserved for Cynar and Aperol, resulting in this perfect after–dinner drink.

GLASSWARE: Rocks glass

GARNISH: Torched orange peel and coffee beans

- 2 oz. Santa Teresa 1796
- ¼ oz. Cynar
- 1 oz. Aperol
- ¼ oz. coffee syrup

1. Combine all ingredients in a cocktail shaker filled with ice and shake.

2. Double–strain over an ice sphere in a rocks glass and garnish with a torched orange peel and coffee beans.

FOR COFFEE SYRUP: In a saucepan, combine equal parts water and sugar. Add coffee beans, using 10 beans per quart of water. Bring to a boil, remove from heat, and let stand for 4 hours. Strain, label, and store.

— WHITE NEGRONI —

CIBO WINEBAR

Ginger liqueur and Grand Marnier bring delicious clarity to this twist on the Negroni.

GLASSWARE: Rocks glass

GARNISH: Lemon twist

- 1 oz. Domaine de Canton liqueur
- 1 oz. Grand Marnier
- 1½ oz. Bulldog Gin

1. Combine all of the ingredients in a mixing glass filled with ice and stir until chilled.

2. Strain into over an ice sphere in a rocks glass and garnish with a lemon twist.

FOR RHUBARB SYRUP: 1 liter of rhubarb puree, 2 liters of sugar, 2 liters of water, and the zest of 2 lemons. Combine all over low heat until sugar is dissolved. Strain and label.

FOR HONEY-GINGER SYRUP: 1 quart honey, 1 quart water, 5⅓ oz. of ginger cut into small pieces and peeled, and 6 oz. of fresh orange juice. Blend together and strain.

FOR CHOCOLATE-INFUSED RUM: Place 2 cups of dark chocolate chips in a 750 ml bottle of rum, infuse for 24 hours, and strain before using.

— HURRICANE —

A Hurricane is one of those cocktails that needs to be perfectly made. Danilo Bozovic's take on it is not only perfect, it also highlights the rums while incorporating flavors not typically found in a traditional Hurricane.

GLASSWARE: Collins glass
GARNISH: Pineapple leaf and brandied cherry

- 1 oz. Plantation Dark Rum
- 1 oz. Banks 5 Island Rum
- ¾ oz. pineapple juice
- ½ oz. fresh lime juice
- ½ oz. rhubarb syrup
- ½ oz. honey-ginger syrup
- ½ oz. grenadine
- Chocolate-infused Don Q 151 Rum, to float

1. Add all ingredients into a mixing glass filled with ice, except the chocolate-infused Don Q 151 Rum, and swizzle to combine.

2. Strain into a Collins glass filled with pebble ice and add more ice until full.

3. Garnish with a pineapple leaf and a brandied cherry, and float the rum on top.

— NEWBURGH SOUR —

EMPLOYEES ONLY

This Danilo Bozovic creation combines scotch, tea, and Amaro balanced with demerara and lemon—a perfect sour to start the evening.

GLASSWARE: Coupe

- 1½ oz. The Glenlivet Founder's Reserve
- ½ oz. black tea–infused Amaro Montenegro
- ¾ oz. demerara syrup
- 1 oz. fresh lemon juice
- 1 egg white
- 3 dashes of Fee Brothers Old Fashioned Bitters
- Nutmeg, to top

1. Combine all ingredients in a cocktail shaker with ice, except the bitters and nutmeg, and shake vigorously.

2. Strain into a coupe.

3. Top with the bitters and freshly grated nutmeg.

FOR BLACK TEA–INFUSED AMARO MONTENGRO: Pour ½ bottle Amaro into pan, add 1 tea bag, and bring to a boil. Add the remaining Amaro and let infuse for 30 minutes.

FOR DEMERARA SYRUP: Combine 2 parts demerara sugar to 1 part water over low heat. Stir occasionally until sugar is dissolved.

— THE BANKS SOUR —

When sipping this drink, whiffs of a bakery will hit you, thanks to the coconut-washed rum, dry-spice syrup, and cherry-cider foam.

GLASSWARE: Nick & Nora glass
GARNISH: Rosemary sprig

- 1½ oz. coconut-washed Banks 7 Golden Age Rum
- ¾ oz. fresh lime juice
- ½ oz. dry-spice syrup
- 5 drops of sage-rosemary tincture
- ½ oz. Cava
- Cherry-cider foam, to top

1. Combine the liquid ingredients, except the Cava and cherry-cider foam, in cocktail shaker.

2. Give a quick, hard shake with ice.

3. Add the Cava and double-strain into a chilled Nick & Nora glass.

4. Top to the rim of glass with cherry-cider foam and garnish with a rosemary sprig.

FOR COCONUT-WASHED BANKS 7: In a large bowl, combine ½ cup unrefined coconut oil with a 750 ml bottle of Banks 7 Golden Age Rum. Stir until well combined and let stand overnight in the freezer. Skim off coconut fat and rebottle.

FOR DRY-SPICE SYRUP: In a saucepan, bring 2 cups of water to a boil and add 3 cinnamon sticks, 3 cloves, and 1 star anise pod. Remove from heat and cover for 3 minutes. Add 3 cups sugar, stir to dissolve, and strain. Label and store.

FOR SAGE-ROSEMARY TINCTURE: Add leaves from 5 sprigs of sage and 5 sprigs of rosemary to 1 cup vodka. Let stand 3 days, strain, and bottle.

FOR CHERRY-CIDER FOAM: In a saucepan, combine 3 cups pitted cherries and 12 oz. Crispin Rosé Cider and simmer on low heat for 20 minutes. Strain and chill. Add 1 teaspoon Versawhip and charge with nitrous oxide in an iSi whipper.

— SALTY DOUG —

GENERATOR HOSTEL MIAMI

This rum riff on a Salty Dog has an incredible mouthfeel, thanks to the Breville Juice Fountain, brought into the mixology realm by bartender Naren Young at the wonderful Caffe Dante in New York City. The juicer spins fast enough to provide additional texture to this cocktail.

GLASSWARE: Collins glass

- 1½ oz. Diplomatico Mantuano Rum
- ½ oz. fresh lime juice
- ¼ oz. agave syrup
- 3 to 4 fresh grapefruits, skin and pith removed, cut into chunks
- Grapefruit salt, for the rim

1. In the juicer cup of Breville Juice Fountain, combine liquid ingredients.

2. Turn juicer on high and add the grapefruit chunks. Wet the rim of a Collins glass and dip it into the grapefruit salt.

3. Swirl to combine, place ice in the glass, and pour the cocktail into it.

FOR AGAVE SYRUP: In a saucepan, combine 3 parts agave nectar to 1 part water. Simmer until desired consistency has been achieved.

FOR GRAPEFRUIT SALT: Take 1 cup of grapefruit pulp left over from the juicer and spread on a sheet in a food dehydrator; run until completely dry. Grind dried pulp in a spice grinder until fine and combine with 1 quart kosher salt.

— KARAJUKU GIMLET —

KAIDO

This beauty from Nico De Soto features the delicately floral kaffir lime cordial playing well with the green tea–infused Mizu Lemongrass Shochu, making for a gorgeously simple and delightful cocktail.

GLASSWARE: Japanese tea glass
GARNISH: Kaffir lime leaves

- 1½ oz. green tea–infused Mizu Lemongrass Shochu
- ¾ oz. kaffir lime cordial

1. Combine all ingredients in a mixing glass filled with ice and stir.

2. Strain into a glass and garnish with kaffir lime leaves.

FOR GREEN TEA–INFUSED MIZU LEMONGRASS SHOCHU: Empty a 750 ml bottle of Mizu Lemongrass Shochu into a large container, add 1 oz. of green tea, and let stand for 8 minutes. Strain the shochu back into the bottle.

FOR KAFFIR LIME CORDIAL: In a saucepan, combine 4 cups water water, 1¼ cups sugar, 2 teaspoons tartaric acid, 1 teaspoon malic acid, and a dash of citric acid and cook until all ingredients are incorporated. Strain, label, store.

— SAYONARA, MOTHERFUCKER! —

KAIDO

This whisky cocktail makes clear why Nico De Soto is an award-winning bartender. The complex Asian-inspired flavors deliver bold umami that lives up to the cocktail's name.

GLASSWARE: Rocks glass

GARNISH: Ichijiku*

- 2 oz. ichijiku-infused Nikka From the Barrel
- 5 drops of white soy sauce
- 2 dashes of kombu and nori bitters
- ⅓ oz. licorice kuromitsu

1. Combine all ingredients in mixing glass over ice and stir.

2. Strain into glass over ice and garnish with sliced ichijiku.

FOR ICHIJIKU INFUSION: Halve 5 ichijiku and combine with a 750 ml bottle of Nikka. Sous vide at 50°C for 1 hour. Let cool. Strain, label, and store.

FOR KOMBU AND NORI BITTERS: Combine a pinch of nori and a dash of kombu with a 6.7 oz. bottle of Angostura Bitters. Sous vide at 52.5°C for 2 hours. Let cool. Strain, label, and store.

FOR LICORICE KUROMITSU: Buy kuromitsu** in market. Let 5 licorice sticks infuse in 1 liter of kuromitsu for 2 weeks. Strain, label, and store.

* Japanese fig

** Japanese sugar syrup (literally, "black honey")

— THE FIFTH ELEMENT —

HABITAT BY JOSE MENDIN

When tequila and avocado come together, you know you're in for a treat. This well-balanced cocktail has a wonderful mouthfeel and the striking color wows guests.

GLASSWARE: Coupe

GARNISH: Dehydrated lemon slice

- 2 oz. Tequila Avión Silver
- 2 oz. avocado mix
- ¾ oz. fresh lime juice
- ½ oz. agave syrup
- 1 egg white
- Citrus salt, for the rim

1. Combine all of the ingredients in a cocktail shaker, fill with ice, and shake until chilled.

2. Wet the rim of a coupe and dip it into the citrus salt.

3. Strain the cocktail into the coupe and garnish with a dehydrated lemon slice.

FOR AVOCADO MIX: Puree 3 avocados, 2 pounds peeled and cored pineapples, and 12 oz. of cilantro.

FOR CITRUS SALT: Zest two lemons and two limes and combine with ½ cup salt.

FOR DEHYDRATED LEMON SLICE: Thinly slice lemons on a deli slicer and arrange on a piece of parchment paper. Insert into dehydrator at 120°F and leave for 12 hours.

— BE MY WINE —

HABITAT BY JOSE MENDIN

Light-bodied rum provides a great base for this exotic cocktail, which is defined by floral notes, spiced citrus from the Falernum, and the white wine reduction.

GLASSWARE: Brandy snifter

GARNISH: Pansies

- 1½ oz. Don Q Rum
- ¾ oz. white wine reduction
- ¾ oz. Velvet Falernum
- 1 spray of lavender oil*

1. Combine all of the ingredients in a mixing glass filled with ice and stir until chilled.

2. Double-strain into the brandy snifter and garnish with pansies.

FOR WHITE WINE REDUCTION: In a saucepan, combine 1 cup of dry white wine with ½ cup of sugar and simmer until reduced by half.

Can be found at specialty stores or online.

— BARRACUDA —

HAKKASAN

The color of this marvelous-looking cocktail comes from the purple potato puree, and the pisco adds complexity that further elevates the unconventional flavors.

GLASSWARE: Rocks glass

GARNISH: Cilantro leaf

- 1½ oz. pisco
- ½ oz. sake
- 1 oz. purple potato puree
- Dash of crushed bird's eye chili
- 2 sprigs of cilantro
- ¼ oz. simple syrup (see page 43)
- ¼ oz. fresh lime juice

1. Place all of the ingredients in a cocktail shaker filled with ice and shake.

2. Double–strain over a large ice cube in a rocks glass.

3. Garnish with a cilantro leaf.

FOR PURPLE POTATO PUREE: Boil 10 to 15 purple potatoes in 4 cups of simple syrup for 5 minutes. Reduce heat to medium–low and cook for 10 minutes. Let cool and puree. Strain, stir, and refrigerate.

— ROOT HEALER —

HAKKASAN

The Root Healer's complex yet delicate Asian-inspired flavors of passion fruit, pear, and tamarind serve as the perfect complement to Hakkasan's incredible Cantonese cuisine.

GLASSWARE: Coupe

- Smoked salt, for the rim
- 1½ oz. pear vodka
- ¼ oz. Calvados VSOP
- ¼ oz. Asian pear puree
- 1 oz. tamarind nectar
- ¼ oz. passion fruit syrup
- ¼ oz. fresh lime juice
- 2 shiso leaves
- ½ oz. simple syrup (see page 43)

1. Wet the rim of a coupe and dip it into the smoked salt. Add all of the remaining ingredients to a cocktail shaker filled with ice and shake vigorously.

2. Double-strain into the coupe.

— PAOMO AMBROSIA —

The cachaça and sake combined with yuzu juice and banana make this complex cocktail effortless to consume.

GLASSWARE: Rocks glass

GARNISH: Powdered white ambrosia tea leaves

- 1½ oz. cachaça
- ½ oz. sake
- 1 oz. banana syrup
- ½ oz. yuzu juice
- ¼ oz. fresh lemon juice
- Crushed shiso leaves
- 1 egg white
- Club soda, to top

1. Combine all ingredients other than the club soda in a cocktail shaker and dry shake.

2. Add ice, shake, and double-strain over ice in a rocks glass.

3. Top with club soda and garnish with the powdered white ambrosia tea leaves.

FOR BANANA SYRUP: Boil 5 peeled ripe bananas in 4 cups of simple syrup (see page 43) for 5 minutes, reduce heat to medium–low, and cook for 15 minutes or until golden brown. Strain and let cool.

— MIAMI SLING PUNCH —

ESOTICO MIAMI

Daniele Dalla Pola riffs on a classic, bringing a signature Sling to the city that packs a "punch" with its perfect blend of citrus and sweet that begs for a second round.

GLASSWARE: Hurricane glass
GARNISH: Pineapple slice, mint sprig, and a cherry

- 2 oz. gin
- ½ oz. Peter Heering Cherry Liqueur
- ½ oz. Reàl Ginger Syrup
- 2 oz. fresh pineapple juice
- ½ oz. Alamea Peach Brandy
- ¾ oz. fresh lime juice
- 2 dashes of Angostura Bitters
- Club soda, to top

1. Combine all ingredients in a cocktail shaker filled with ice and shake vigorously.

2. Strain over fresh ice in a tall glass, top with club soda, and garnish with a slice of pineapple, mint sprig, and a cherry; an orchid blossom is optional.

— KAMA'AINA —

With the opening of Esotico Miami, Daniele Dalla Pola finally brings his tiki vibes stateside. This exotic, pleasant medley of rums and tropical fruits will make your eyes roll. Say hello to tiki!

GLASSWARE: Empty coconut or a tall glass
GARNISH: Orchid blossom

- 1 oz. Alamea Spiced Rum
- 1 oz. Rhum Agricole
- 1 oz. guava nectar
- ½ oz. #9

- ½ oz. Reàl Cream of Coconut
- ½ oz. fresh lime juice
- 2 dashes of Angostura Bitters

1. Combine all ingredients, except the bitters, in a cocktail shaker filled with crushed ice and shake until chilled.

2. Pour unstrained into glass, add bitters, and garnish with an orchid blossom.

FOR #9: Combine 2 oz. Reàl Ginger Syrup with 1 oz. almond paste and blend, then add one spoonful of Alamea Pimento Liqueur.

— DAN'S PIÑA PARADISE —

ESOTICO MIAMI

Daniele Dalla Pola has dug into the history books for this tiki beauty that will now be part of Esotico Miami's permanent menu. Jack Kofoed writes in *Moon Over Miami*, "Because of its geographical location and clime, Miami has taken on the lure of a modern-day tropical isle. Befitting this concept, this resort town has discovered that exotic potions are becoming increasingly popular. Number one on the sip parade is a tasty beverage originated here in Miami." This original recipe comes from Sam Denning of Club Luau, a popular spot in Miami during the 1950s.

GLASSWARE: Brandy snifter
GARNISH: Cinnamon and strips of orange peel

- 2 oz. Bacardi Añejo Cuatro Rum
- ½ oz. Plantation Pineapple Rum
- 1½ oz. citrus mix
- 1 oz. #9 (see page 159)
- 4 chunks of fresh pineapple

1. Combine all ingredients in a blender with crushed ice.

2. Pour unstrained into a brandy snifter and garnish with cinnamon and strips of orange peel.

FOR CITRUS MIX: Combine equal parts fresh lime juice, grapefruit juice, and orange juice.

REMEMBER TO EAT!

All the amazing local ingredients don't just make for exciting cocktails, and the food in Miami should not be missed. Check out any of these favorites to find out why.

MONTY'S is a staple in Coconut Grove. Opened in 1969, this waterfront tiki hut serves fresh seafood with a happy hour raw bar. Walk on in and order yourself a Pain Remover—a Monty's classic made from a blend of Virgin Island Rum, coconut cream, pineapple juice, and orange juice. On top of the delicious food and drink, Monty's also has an incredible view.

Have you tried the burger at **TAURUS BEER & WHISK(E)Y HOUSE**? It is incredible and priced to sell. Their selection of whiskey and local beers is equally impressive and sure to get you in the mood for one of their famous trivia nights.

SHUCKERS WATERFRONT GRILL has been open for over 25 years and offers great seafood and bites. Situated on the island of North Bay Village in the heart of Biscayne Bay, the view is what really keeps the locals coming back.

HAPPY WINE, now with two locations, is a local tapas bar where you can relax with some small bites and drink the wine you purchased at their shop. Take a seat on an oak barrel and enjoy some Spanish-style tapas with your favorite bottle.

19TH HOLE BAR AND GRILL is located at the historic Biltmore Hotel in Coral Gables. The hotel was opened in 1926 and doubled as a military hospital in World War II. This property sits amidst the oak-lined residential streets of Coral Gables and provides a perfect view to enjoy some wine and eats.

PUBBELLY mastered the art of small plates in Miami Beach, and has transformed into a noodle bar with craft beer and fine wine. A must stop.

The **UNION BEER STORE** is a craft beer haven in the heart of Little Havana that has plenty of delicious eats to pair with their numerous drafts.

EL EXQUISITO is located right in the center of Miami's Little Havana. You can expect to find traditional Cuban dishes and sandwiches, but make sure you save room for the Cuban pastries and a cafecito.

REY DE LAS FRITAS is the home of the Cuban Hamburger, known as the "frita." The original frita was brought over by Dagoberto Estevil in 1961, and you won't find any finer in all of Miami.

ARIETE puts Chef Michael Beltran's food at the forefront of Coconut Grove's culinary scene. Here you can find American fare with a Cuban flair. Chef Beltran's fritas and hamburgers are award-winning, and his cocktails are always constructed with fresh local ingredients.

FINKA TABLE AND TAP is Chef Eileen Andrade's love letter to West Miami. This gastropub introduced the neighborhood to fresh ingredients and progressive menu items, including Cuban food with Asian and Latin American influences. Definitely worth the trip.

MACCHIALINA is the brainchild of a husband–and–wife team, Chef Mike Pirolo and Jennifer Chaefsky, who have brought rustic Italian food in an intimate setting to Miami Beach. This is arguably the best Italian food in Miami and the service is James Beard Award-worthy.

LIDO BAYSIDE GRILL AT THE STANDARD is our home away from Miami Beach—though it is located in Miami Beach. Sit back and enjoy a glass of Rosé while sampling some light bites. An industry favorite, the restaurant sits bayside and provides breathtaking views of the city.

LA SANDWICHERIE has two locations, but their location across from Mac's Club Deuce in Miami Beach is memorable. They are famous for their late-night sandwiches and, of course, don't forget their magic sauce. You can count on enjoying your favorite sandwich until 5:00 a.m., as this late-night spot has been open for over 30 years.

BURGER MUSEUM BY BURGER BEAST is a must while in Miami. The 2,300–square foot Burger Museum and Wall's Old Fashioned Ice Cream Shop feature over 3,000 pieces of historical artifacts, collectibles, and ephemera. Love burgers? Stop by and get ready to get schooled on the juicy history of America's favorite meal.

— JULIO CALIENTE —

JUVIA

The rooftop at Juvia offers up one of the most postcard–perfect views in Miami Beach, and this tasty cocktail is just as stunning. Bringing in Peruvian influences from the kitchen, the aji amarillo plays perfectly off the fresh watermelon juice.

GLASSWARE: Collins or highball glass

GARNISH: Watermelon slice

- 1½ oz. Don Julio Blanco
- ½ oz. aji amarillo–infused Aperol
- 1½ oz. fresh watermelon juice
- ¼ oz. fresh lime juice
- 1 oz. fresh guava
- ½ oz. watermelon syrup

1. Combine all of the ingredients in a cocktail shaker filled with ice and shake vigorously.

2. Strain over ice in a glass and garnish with a watermelon slice.

— CAPRIRINHA —

The combination of limoncello and cachaça puts an Italian twist on a Brazilian classic.

GLASSWARE: **Rocks glass**

- ½ oz. fresh lime juice
- ¼ oz. simple syrup (see page 43)
- 1 slice of fresh ginger
- ¾ oz. Avua Cachaça
- ¾ oz. Limoncello di Capri
- Dash of Crème de Mure

1. Place the lime, simple syrup, and ginger in a rocks glass and muddle.

2. Add ice, the cachaça, and limoncello and stir.

3. Finish with a dash of Crème de Mure.

— SICILIAN PISCO —

LA MODERNA

Pisco in an Italian joint? Don't worry, you'll find that the Bénédictine and pisco are best friends in this stunning spicy cocktail.

GLASSWARE: Coupe

GARNISH: Rosemary sprig

- 1½ oz. pisco
- ¼ oz. Vecchio Amaro Del Capo
- 1 slice of jalapeño pepper
- ½ oz. Bénédictine
- ¼ oz. fresh lemon juice

1. Combine all of the ingredients in a cocktail shaker filled with ice and shake vigorously.

2. Strain into a coupe and garnish with a sprig of fresh rosemary.

— TROPIC PUNCH —

LIVING ROOM AT THE W HOTEL

The tropical flavors of this punch are right at home on the sands of Miami Beach.

GLASSWARE: Tall glass

GARNISH: Ground nutmeg

- 2 oz. dark rum
- ½ oz. Aperol
- 1 oz. pineapple juice
- 1 oz. orange juice
- ¾ oz. fresh lime juice
- ¾ oz. agave syrup
- Dash of egg white

1. Combine all ingredients in a cocktail shaker filled with ice and shake vigorously.

2. Strain over ice in a glass and garnish with ground nutmeg.

— LA BANDOLERA —

The lavender and citrus make this tequila-champagne cocktail shine. Perfect for day drinking!

GLASSWARE: Champagne flute

GARNISH: Long strip of lemon peel

- 1 oz. blanco tequila
- ½ oz. lavender syrup
- ½ oz. fresh lemon juice
- 2 dashes of Bittermens Hopped Grapefruit Bitters
- Prosecco, to top

1. Combine all ingredients, except the Prosecco, in a cocktail shaker filled with ice and shake vigorously.

2. Strain into a champagne flute, top with Prosecco, and garnish with a long strip of lemon peel.

FOR LAVENDER SYRUP: In a saucepan, combine 1 cup of water, 1 cup of sugar, and 1 tablespoon of lavender blossoms and bring to a boil. Simmer until sugar is dissolved, and then let cool for 1 hour. Label and store.

— CHAVELA MICHELADA —

LOLO'S SURF CANTINA

The Michelada is becoming a well-loved cocktail in Miami. I love this delicious tangy version beachside when I'm enjoying some fish tacos!

GLASSWARE: Pint glass

GARNISH: Lime wedge

- Tajin,* for the rim
- 1 oz. Chavela Mexican Mix
- 2 oz. tomato juice
- ¾ oz. lime juice
- Pacifico Beer, to top

1. Wet the rim of a pint glass and dip it into the Tajin.

2. Place the Chavela Mexican Mix, tomato juice, and lime juice in the pint glass, add ice, and top with the Pacifico.

3. Garnish with a lime wedge.

FOR CHAVELA MEXICAN MIX: Combine a dash of Valentina, a dash of Maggi, dash of Worcestershire sauce, and 1 oz. tomato juice.

This blend of chili peppers, salt, and dehydrated lime is used to season fruit, candy, and vegetables, and gives your cocktail the kick it deserves.

LOLO'S
SURF CANTINA

— BIG TROUBLE IN LITTLE CHIANTO SPRITZ —

MACCHIALINA

Spritzes are an ideal Miami cocktail. This low-ABV concoction can be made quickly and built in the glass. Share this one with friends or enjoy at Macchialina, one of Miami's best Italian restaurants.

GLASSWARE: Wine glass
GARNISH: Grapefruit twist

- 1 oz. Giulio Cocchi
- 1 oz. Barolo Chianto
- 2 oz. Q Grapefruit Soda
- 1 oz. Lovo Prosecco

1. Combine all ingredients in a wine glass, add ice, and stir to blend.

2. Garnish with a grapefruit twist.

— THE SPECK–TACULAR NOW —

MACCHIALINA

You had me at speck! This take on an Old Fashioned features speck-infused bourbon, which plays well with the playful complexity of honey-clove syrup.

GLASSWARE: Rocks glass
GARNISH: Strip of orange peel

- 2 oz. speck–infused Old Forester bourbon
- ½ oz. honey–clove syrup
- Dash of Bittercube Jamaican #1 Bitters

1. Place all of the ingredients in a mixing glass filled with ice and stir until chilled.

2. Strain over ice in a rocks glass and garnish with a strip of orange peel.

FOR SPECK–INFUSED BOURBON: Render the speck fat in a skillet. Add 8 oz. of fat per bottle and vacuum seal. Sous vide at 155°F for 1½ hours. Placed the cooked liquor into quart containers and freeze overnight. Scrape the fat off and double-strain through a fine sieve and cheesecloth.

FOR HONEY–CLOVE SYRUP: In a saucepan, combine 2 cups honey and 2 cups water and bring to a boil while stirring. Remove the pan from heat, add 25 whole cloves, and steep at room temperature until cool. Strain out cloves, label, and store.

MOVERS & SHAKERS:

Joshua Wagner managed The Florida Room at the beginning of Miami's cocktail revolution and went on to become Director of Culture and Entertainment at Edition, where he continues to push the boundaries of the bar.

— THE PINEAPPLE —

MATADOR ROOM AT THE EDITION HOTEL, MIAMI BEACH

The Pineapple, defined by the house-made pineapple mix, is one of Matador Room's signature cocktails, and is served in a stunning vessel.

GLASSWARE: Copper pineapple
GARNISH: Torched rosemary sprig

- 2½ oz. Absolut Elyx
- 2 oz. pineapple mix
- 1 oz. pineapple puree
- ¾ oz. fresh lemon juice
- Peychaud's Bitters, to top

1. Combine all of the ingredients, except the bitters, in a cocktail shaker filled with ice and shake until chilled.

2. Fill a copper pineapple with crushed ice, strain the cocktail over the ice, and add more crushed ice until full.

3. Add Peychaud's Bitters until layered on top of cocktail and then garnish with a torched rosemary sprig.

FOR PINEAPPLE MIX: Combine 1¼ cups Oloroso Sherry, ½ cup Salted Vanilla Syrup (see below), 1 cup rosemary syrup (see page 67), ½ cup pineapple puree, ½ cup simple syrup (see page 43), and ½ bottle Bittermens 'Elemakule Tiki Bitters. Mix, label, and refrigerate.

FOR SALTED VANILLA SYRUP: In a saucepan over low heat, combine 3 pinches of salt, 2 cups simple syrup, and 1 tablespoon vanilla extract. Simmer until salt has dissolved.

— COPPER CUP #4 —

Another Matador Room favorite is the Cooper Cup #4. The fresh ginger keeps you alert so you can take in the surroundings at this gorgeous bar.

GLASSWARE: Copper cup

GARNISH: Ginger slice and an orchid blossom

- 2 oz. Absolut Elyx
- ¾ oz. St–Germain
- ¼ oz. fresh ginger juice
- ¾ oz. fresh lemon juice
- ¼ oz. hibiscus syrup

1. Combine all of the ingredients in a cocktail shaker filled with ice and shake until chilled.

2. Strain the cocktail into a copper cup filled with ice and top off with more crushed ice.

3. Garnish with a ginger slice and an orchid blossom.

MOVERS & SHAKERS:

Angelo Vieira is one of those bartenders who makes you fall in love with bartending. Never one to demand the limelight despite his tremendous abilities, Vieira is one of the world's best bartenders and can be found serving up classics and providing incredible service at the Matador Room.

Dennis Luna has been contributing to Miami's cocktail scene for years and proudly calls Miami home. One of those bartenders who makes the world go round, he happily serves up incredible cocktails with a smile at Matador Room.

— CHARCOAL BOURBON SOUR —

PLANTA SOUTH BEACH

Activated charcoal is a fairly new cocktail ingredient and should be used sparingly to add dramatic color. Between that and the aquafaba,* this drink is innovation in a glass.

GLASSWARE: Tulip glass
GARNISH: Dried flower

- 1½ oz. Four Roses Small Batch Bourbon
- 1 oz. aquafaba
- 1 oz. fresh lemon juice
- 1 oz. activated charcoal syrup

1. Place all of the ingredients in a cocktail shaker filled with ice and shake vigorously.

2. Strain into a tulip glass and garnish with a dried flower.

FOR ACTIVATED CHARCOAL SYRUP: Bring 2½ cups water to boil. Add 2½ cups sugar. Once sugar is dissolved, add 8 oz. charcoal powder mix and let cool. Label and store.

Some people don't eat eggs; some mixologists eat eggs but don't like the smell they impart to cocktails. This vegan egg substitute has been all the rage with pastry chefs for years and now it is being folded into drink recipes. Easiest way to source it? You can make it by boiling chickpeas and skimming off the foam, or just open up a can of chickpeas, pour the liquid into a container, label, and store.

— PRINCESS AND THE FROG —

Lavender bitters keep this delicate combination from being too floral, and the St–Germain imparts wonderful depth.

GLASSWARE: Rocks glass

GARNISH: Basil leaf and a gummy frog

- 1½ oz. EG Inspiration Vodka
- ¾ oz. fresh lemon juice
- ¾ oz. blueberry–basil syrup
- ½ oz. St–Germain
- 2 dashes of Scrappy's Lavender Bitters

1. Place all of the ingredients in a cocktail shaker filled with ice and shake until chilled. Strain over a cube of ice in a rocks glass.

2. Garnish with a basil leaf and a gummy frog.

FOR BLUEBERRY–BASIL SYRUP: In a saucepan, combine 4 cups sugar with 4 cups water and bring to a boil, stirring occasionally. Add 2 cups blueberries and 8 to 10 basil leaves and let simmer for 10 minutes. Let cool, strain, and store.

FOR GUMMY FROG: Start with 1 Jello packet and prepare according to manufacturer's instructions, but with only half the water. Add 2 tablespoons Knox Gelatin Powder and stir until powder has integrated with liquid. Pour into frog molds (or molds of your choice) and place in fridge for 1 hour, or until hardened.

MOVERS & SHAKERS:

Isaac Grillo is no stranger to the bar community here in Miami, having worked at DeVito's and Haven before opening his own bar, Repour Bar, in the lobby of the Albion Hotel. They serve cocktails with a culinary twist that have been enjoyed for years, and Grillo continues to mentor bartenders at Repour while working on opening his new bar, Death & Glory, in Delray Beach.

— M. I. A. M. I. (MONEY IS A MAJOR ISSUE) —

REPOUR BAR

Passion fruit liqueur and lavender bitters highlight the citrusy botanicals in this local gin, making for a sour cocktail that is both easy to drink and gorgeous.

GLASSWARE: Coupe

GARNISH: Orchid blossom, or any edible flower

- 1½ oz. Big Cypress Magic City Gin
- ¾ oz. fresh lemon juice
- ½ oz. simple syrup (see page 43)
- ½ oz. grapefruit juice
- ½ oz. Giffard Passion Fruit Liqueur
- Dash of Scrappy's Lavender Bitters
- 1 egg white

1. Place all of the ingredients in cocktail shaker filled with ice, shake until chilled, and strain. Discard the ice, return the cocktail to the shaker, and shake for the perfect egg white foam.

2. Strain into the coupe and garnish with an orchid blossom, or any type of edible flower.

— AVELLINO —

SCARPETTA

There is a surprisingly wonderful balance in how hoppy Lagunitas IPA brings together the tropical, herbaceous, and floral citrus notes in this beer cocktail.

GLASSWARE: Tulip glass

GARNISH: Green apple slices and a cardamom pod

- 1 lemon wedge, for the rim
- Pistachio–cardamom powdered sugar, for the rim
- ½ green apple, chopped
- ¼ oz. pineapple syrup
- ¼ oz. yuzu juice
- ¼ oz. pineapple juice
- ½ oz. Chartreuse
- 1½ oz. Plantation Pineapple Rum
- Lagunitas IPA, to top

1. Wet the rim of the tulip glass with the lemon wedge and dip it into the pistachio–cardamom powdered sugar. Place a large ice cube in the glass.

2. Muddle the green apple in a cocktail shaker and then add ice. Place all of the remaining ingredients, except the beer, in the shaker and shake to combine.

3. Double–strain into the tulip glass and top with IPA.

4. Garnish with 3 slices of green apple and a cardamom pod.

FOR PISTACHIO–CARDAMOM POWDERED SUGAR: Combine equal parts ground cardamom, powdered sugar, and crushed pistachios.

FOR PINEAPPLE SYRUP: Bring 1 quart of water to a boil. Add 1 pineapple, chopped, and 1 guajillo pepper and simmer for 20 minutes. Add 1 quart of granulated sugar and stir until sugar has dissolved. Let simmer for 5 minutes. Remove from heat, strain through a fine sieve, and store.

— MANGO —

SCARPETTA

This mango-kumquat puree makes tropical magic with the complex combination of rhum, cognac, and Amaro.

GLASSWARE: Pilsner glass
GARNISH: Dried mango slice and a kumquat slice

- 1½ oz. mango–kumquat puree
- ¼ oz. Rhum Clément Créole Shrubb
- ¾ oz. Velvet Falernum
- ¾ oz. Amaro Montenegro
- ¾ oz. Hennessey VSOP
- Brachetto, to top

1. Place all of the ingredients, except the Brachetto, in a cocktail shaker filled with ice and shake.

2. Double-strain into a pilsner glass, top with Brachetto, and add ice.

3. Garnish with a dried mango slice and a kumquat slice.

FOR MANGO–KUMQUAT PUREE: Peel 2 mangoes, chop, and add to blender; chop, remove seeds from ⅔ quart of kumquats, and add to blender. Juice 4 oranges and add juice to blender. Add ½ quart of water to blender and puree contents until silky.

KEEP IT LOCAL

While Miami's cocktail and beer communities have continued to grow, we have seen more growth on the brewery side than the distillery side. There are many distilleries in Florida, but there is only one making serious rum in Miami. We have highlighted that distillery below and added the profiles of two other breweries in the area.

BIG CYPRESS DISTILLERY

Founded in 2015, Big Cypress Distillery was started by like-minded family members. Inspired by today's craft movement, they reminisced about their love of their hometown, Miami, Florida. With self–taught distiller Fernando Plata leading production, Big Cypress began creating gin and rum. Fernando has spent countless hours studying books dating back to the 1600s to gain a better understanding and hone his craft. Today, Fernando has created a wide array of spirits with integrity, including the gin and rum. He has also created special editions of his productions while working to educate the community on local craft spirits.

J. WAKEFIELD BREWING

Jonathan Wakefield opened the doors to J. Wakefield Brewing in January 2015 after some home brewing experience and a quick stop at Cigar City Brewing. Based in Wynwood, the design of the brewery plays off the artsy neighborhood's décor with murals adorning the walls. Their beers can be found all over Miami, with special releases highly coveted by beer aficionados.

THE TANK BREWING CO.

The Tank is housed in a 25,000-square foot warehouse in Doral. Looking to create exceptional beer with a hint of Miami, the brewery's offerings have already won numerous awards and continue to move the needle on what can be produced in Miami. The team is made up of home brewers and a cigar industry veteran who wanted to introduce Miami to a whole new way to drink beer.

— SOUTH OF 5TH SMASH —

SOUTH POINTE TAVERN

South Pointe is one of those bars built with a lot of love, and the cocktails are no different. The Oloroso Sherry brings this one together while raspberry preserves provide the backbone, making for a great pre–dinner drink.

GLASSWARE: Goblet

GARNISH: Lime wheel and a blackberry

- 1 oz. Oloroso Sherry
- 1 oz. Cedilla Açai Liqueur
- ½ oz. fresh lime juice
- ½ oz. fresh lemon juice
- ½ oz. simple syrup (see page 43)
- 4 basil leaves

1. Combine all of the ingredients in a mixing glass filled with ice and stir until chilled.

2. Strain over ice in a goblet and garnish with a lime wheel and a blackberry.

— MIAMI STATE OF MIND —

SOUTH POINTE TAVERN

Spicy, sweet, and to top it all off, fresh watermelon juice—a Miami staple!

GLASSWARE: Collins or highball glass
GARNISH: Ground pepper and a lime wheel

- 1½ oz. blanco tequila
- ½ oz. agave syrup
- ½ oz. fresh lime juice
- 1½ oz. fresh watermelon juice
- Pinch of cilantro
- Pinch of jalapeño pepper, minced

1. Combine all of the ingredients in a mixing glass filled with ice and stir until chilled.

2. Strain over ice in a glass and garnish with ground pepper and a lime wheel.

— RHUM SWIZZLE —

SWIZZLE

The funky rhum plays with the watermelon shrub in this Danilo Bozovic cocktail—a perfect summer sipper at the Washington Park Hotel in Miami Beach.

GLASSWARE: Tiki glass

GARNISH: Watermelon slice

- 1½ oz. Rhum JM 100 Proof
- 1 oz. watermelon shrub
- ½ oz. freshly squeezed lime juice
- ½ oz. simple syrup (see page 43)
- ½ oz. pineapple juice

1. Place all of the ingredients and some pebble ice in a tiki glass.

2. Stir in glass until blended and chilled.

3. Add ice to top and garnish with a watermelon slice.

FOR WATERMELON SHRUB: Combine the juice from 1 pressed watermelon with equal parts apple cider vinegar and sugar (usually 2 cups vinegar and 2 cups sugar).

— BANANA DAIQUIRI —

SWIZZLE

Banana Daiquiris should be celebrated all over the world. Danilo Bozovic's incredibly refreshing version is an attempt to make that happen, hitting a perfectly delicious balance of flavors.

GLASSWARE: Coupe

GARNISH: Angostura Bitters and a banana chip

- 2 oz. Parce 3–Year Rum
- 1½ oz. banana puree
- ½ oz. simple syrup (see page 43)
- ¼ oz. fresh lime juice

1. Place all of the ingredients and ½ cup ice in a blender and puree until combined.

2. Pour into a coupe and top with 3 dashes of Angostura Bitters and a banana chip.

— MANNY'S BLUE JEANS —

STRIPSTEAK BY MICHAEL MINA

This twist on a margarita features delicious Chinola Passion Fruit Liqueur paired with tangy Tajin, making for a perfect blend of citrus that honors the original margarita.

GLASSWARE: Rocks glass
GARNISH: Tajin–dipped lime wheel

- 1 lime wedge, for the rim
- Tajin, for the rim
- 1 oz. Revolucion Tequila
- 1 oz. Chinola Passion Fruit Liqueur

- ½ oz. fresh lime juice
- ½ oz. agave syrup

1. Wet the rim of a rocks glass with the lime wedge and dip it into the Tajin.

2. Combine all of the remaining ingredients in a cocktail shaker filled with ice and shake.

3. Strain over ice into the rocks glass.

4. Garnish with a Tajin–dipped lime wheel.

— GO AHEAD ROMEO —

STRIPSTEAK BY MICHAEL MINA

This very simple preparation is a stunning addition to any cocktail party. Aperol almost glows when it's frozen, and as it starts to melt the citrus notes add another layer to the Prosecco. Don't be afraid to use these Aperol ice cubes for other cocktails as well.

GLASSWARE: Brandy snifter
GARNISH: Orange twist

- **6 Aperol ice cubes**
- **4 oz. Prosecco**

1. Put Aperol ice cubes in a brandy snifter and add Prosecco.

2. Garnish with a long orange twist.

FOR APEROL ICE CUBES: The ratio is ¼ Aperol to ¾ water; freeze in ice cube trays.

— THYME TRAVELER —

STUBBORN SEED

This drink tastes like summer with gin, elderflower, and cucumber combined with citrus and spicy bitters. The thyme syrup ties it all together, highlighting the botanicals in the gin.

GLASSWARE: Highball glass
GARNISH: Thyme and sliced cucumber

- 1½ oz. Bombay Dry Gin
- ½ oz. St-Germain
- ¾ oz. fresh pressed cucumber juice
- ½ oz. thyme syrup
- ½ oz. lemon juice
- Dash of Bittermens Hellfire Habanero Bitters

1. Combine all ingredients in a cocktail shaker filled with ice and shake vigorously.

2. Strain over ice into a highball glass and garnish with thyme and sliced cucumber.

FOR THYME SYRUP: In a saucepan, combine 1 cup of water, 1 cup of sugar, and 1 small bundle of thyme and bring to a boil. Simmer until sugar is dissolved, and then let cool for 1 hour. Label and store.

— DESERT DAISY —

STUBBORN SEED

This stunning tequila cocktail is served in handmade glass and combines bell peppers, beets, saline, and Amaro for a complex cocktail sure to wow your guests.

GLASSWARE: Quido Jakobsen Glass, or rocks glass
GARNISH: Carrot-habanero powder and an edible flower

- 1½ oz. Olmeca Altos Tequila Plata
- ½ oz. Brovo Amaro #4
- ¾ oz. fresh lime juice
- ¾ oz. orange bell pepper and beet syrup
- 4 drops of 25 percent saline solution
- 10 dashes of Bittermens Hellfire Habanero Bitters

1. Combine all ingredients in a cocktail shaker filled with ice and shake vigorously.

2. Strain over ice in the chosen glassware and garnish with carrot-habanero powder and an edible flower.

FOR ORANGE BELL PEPPER AND BEET SYRUP: Juice ½ cup of orange bell pepper and ½ cup of beets separately, and strain remaining pulp from each one. In a saucepan, combine juices and add 1 cup sugar. Bring to a boil and then simmer until sugar is dissolved. Let cool for 30 minutes. Label and store.

FOR 25 PERCENT SALINE SOLUTION: Add 1 oz. of salt to measuring glass. Add water until you reach 4 oz. and the salt is dissolved. Do not add water by measurement as the salt will change the volume of the solution.

FOR CARROT-HABANERO POWDER: Combine equal parts of dehydrated carrots, chili flakes, and salt. Blend together. Label and store.

— PIÑA COLADA —

You haven't tried a Piña Colada until you've tried the recipe from legendary bartender John Lermayer. The perfect blend of rum, coconut, citrus, and coffee (yes, coffee!), topped off with a PX sherry float.

GLASSWARE: Hurricane glass or foot–long glass
GARNISH: Maraschino cherry, flamingo pick,
cocktail umbrella, and a mint bouquet

- 2 oz. Secret Rum Blend
- 2 oz. fresh pineapple juice
- 1 oz. Coco Real
- ¼ oz. fresh lemon juice
- 3 coffee beans
- ½ oz. Lustau PX Sherry, to float

1. Combine all of the ingredients, except the sherry, in the glass with ice.

2. Float the sherry on top and garnish with a maraschino cherry, flamingo pick, umbrella, and a mint bouquet.

FOR SECRET RUM BLEND: It's a blend of overproof, Jamaican, and Venezuelan rums. The exact recipe is a highly guarded industry secret, so tinker until you find a mix that's to your liking!

— ROCKAWAY DAIQUIRI —

SWEET LIBERTY DRINKS & SUPPLY CO.

John Lermayer, with the help of barman Nick Nistico, devised what could be the best Daiquiri on the planet. The texture, the balance, the taste, the aroma—it's all spot on. A perfect Miami sipper.

GLASSWARE: Coupe

GARNISH: Freshly grated nutmeg

- 1 oz. Jamaican rum
- 1 oz. Venezuelan rum
- 2 oz. fresh pineapple juice
- ¾ oz. Licor 43
- ½ oz. agave syrup
- 2 drops of aromatic bitters

1. Combine all of the ingredients in a cocktail shaker filled with ice cubes and shake vigorously.

2. Double-strain into a coupe and garnish with freshly grated nutmeg.

IN MEMORIAM:

Over the course of Miami cocktail history, no one has had more of an impact than John Lermayer, as you saw in the intro to this book. He helped champion the cocktail revival in Miami that brought fresh ingredients, incredible cocktails, and amazing bartenders to this growing community. It is impossible to summarize his contributions to the Miami cocktail scene here, as his legacy deserves a book of its own. John came to Miami to bartend at the SkyBar in the Shore Club. His bar had fresh ingredients (an uncommon sight in Miami at the time) and his seamless style behind the bar would carry throughout his career. When he led the bar team at The Florida Room, guests were drinking Mules, Manhattans, and Old Fashioneds—forgotten cocktails in Miami's bars and restaurants at the time. Many hospitality professionals—myself included—mark John's time at The Florida Room as a turning point in Miami's cocktail revolution. John's bottomless thirst for knowledge led him all over the world, meeting bartenders and ambassadors who would come to Miami and return the favor. John was a great leader in the world of spirits, and his colleagues recognized that. John, along with his trusted bar team, went on to open the award–winning Regent Cocktail Club, which championed classic cocktails on its menu. After his stint at the Regent Cocktail Club, he turned his attention to his masterwork, Sweet Liberty. His work and mentorship quickly brought Sweet Liberty worldwide recognition and numerous awards. John always went out of his way to make you feel welcomed and he helped give Miami a place at the table with other major cocktail destinations. He will be remembered as an incredible bartender, a trusted educator and mentor, a loving father, and a devoted friend. He cared about the people he surrounded himself with and was an extraordinary human being.

— SOUTH POINTE SWIZZLE —

UPLAND

This beautifully refreshing take on a Margarita was inspired by the color of the sand used in the bull rings at the wonderful Matador Room in Miami Beach.

GLASSWARE: Collins or highball glass
GARNISH: Mint bouquet and lemongrass syrup

- 2 oz. Bacardi Superior
- 1 oz. fresh lime juice
- ¾ oz. lemongrass syrup
- Pinch of mint leaves
- Dash of Angostura Bitters

1. Combine all of the ingredients, except the bitters, in a Collins glass.

2. Add crushed ice and mix using a swizzle stick* until all ingredients are combined.

3. Add crushed ice to fill and top with a dash of bitters.

4. Garnish with a mint bouquet and lemongrass syrup.

FOR LEMONGRASS SYRUP: In a saucepan, combine 1 cup of water and 1 cup sugar and bring to a boil, stirring until sugar is dissolved. Remove from heat, add 2 coarsely chopped lemongrass stalks, and let steep for 24 hours. Strain, label, and store.

This can be found at specialty barware stores and is used by rubbing both hands together as the stick revolves, creating a mixing pattern.

COCONUT

GROVE

The oldest neighborhood in Miami, dating back to 1825, Coconut Grove became known for its bohemian proclivities. This village by the bay boasts great restaurants, art galleries, and a walkable area full of parks and sidewalk cafés.

— CHUG'S OLD FASHIONED —

ARIETE

Substituting maple syrup for simple syrup, Ariete's riff on an Old Fashioned adds a bit of decadence that stands up well to the tobacco notes in this drink.

GLASSWARE: Rocks glass

GARNISH: Strip of orange peel

- 2 oz. Four Roses bourbon
- ¼ oz. tobacco–infused maple syrup
- 3 dashes of sour orange bitters

1. Place all of the ingredients in a mixing glass filled with ice and stir until chilled.

2. Strain over large cube of ice in a rocks glass.

3. Express the orange peel over glass and add as garnish.

FOR TOBACCO–INFUSED MAPLE SYRUP: Place maple syrup in a pot and bring to a boil. Throw in a pinch of shredded tobacco leaves and stir until flavor and essence is infused. Strain and chill.

FOR SOUR ORANGE BITTERS: Remove peels of 1 navel orange, 2 blood oranges, and 7 sour oranges. Combine the peels, 2 cups Everclear, ½ cup Sherry La Gitana, 2 tablespoons demerara syrup, 8 cardamon pods, 1 tablespoon coriander seeds, and 4 allspice berries. Steep for 6 days, double–strain through cheesecloth, label, and store.

— GREEN PARROT —

ARIETE

This is a riff on Jörg Meyer's (Le Lion in Hamburg) modern classic, the Gin Basil Smash. Here the difference is in the "Secret Sweetness," which adds hints of molasses that make the gin shine.

GLASSWARE: Rocks glass
GARNISH: Basil leaf

- **2 oz. basil–infused Hendrick's Gin**
- **½ oz. lemon juice**
- **½ oz. Secret Sweetness**

1. Place all of the ingredients in a cocktail shaker filled with ice.

2. Shake until cold and double–strain over ice in a rocks glass.

3. Garnish with a basil leaf.

FOR BASIL–INFUSED GIN: Using fresh basil leaves, add 15 to 20 ripped leaves to a gin–filled mason jar. Steep for a week, strain, and label.

FOR SECRET SWEETNESS: Combine equal parts demerara sugar and water. Simmer over low heat and stir occasionally until the sugar is dissolved.

— LA MULA —

GLASS & VINE

G lass & Vine cocktails are a perfect complement to Chef Giorgio Rapicavoli's menu. La Mula is a refreshingly spicy, ginger-forward take on a Mule.

GLASSWARE: Rocks glass

GARNISH: Chili peppers

- 1½ oz. Olmeca Altos Tequila Plata
- ½ oz. Domaine de Canton
- 1 oz. fresh lime juice
- 4 slices of jalapeño pepper
- 4 oz. ginger beer, to top

1. Combine all of the ingredients in a cocktail shaker filled with ice, except the ginger beer, and shake vigorously.

2. Double–strain over ice into a rocks glass, top with ginger beer, and garnish with two chili peppers.

— GIN BLOSSOM —

GLASS & VINE

The floral delights of the Gin Blossom make the views of Peacock Park that much better.

GLASSWARE: Rocks glass
GARNISH: Edible flower and a strip of grapefruit peel

- 1½ oz. Bombay Sapphire Gin
- ½ oz. St–Germain
- ½ oz. Giffard Crème de Pamplemousse Rose
- 1 oz. fresh lemon juice
- Splash of tonic water

1. Combine all of the ingredients in a cocktail shaker filled with ice, except the tonic, and shake vigorously.

2. Strain over ice into a rocks glass, add the tonic, and garnish with an edible flower and a strip of grapefruit peel.

— PAIN REMOVER —

Monty's in Coconut Grove has been serving up tropical cocktails since 1969, and Miamians still love their great happy hours and breathtaking views of the bay. The Pain Remover is a local favorite, served as #1, #2, or #3, depending on how much rum you want in it.

GLASSWARE: Plastic cup

- 1½ oz. rum
- ½ oz. coconut cream
- 2 oz. orange juice
- 12 oz. pineapple juice

Combine all of the ingredients in a cocktail shaker filled with ice, shake vigorously, and pour into a plastic cup.

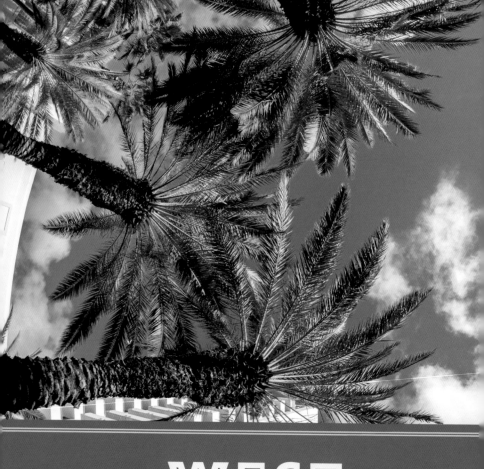

WEST

KENDALL

West Kendall, as the name indicates, is west of Miami's city center and is considered more of a suburban area. Many eateries have sprung up and great Cuban food can be found in these parts. Craft cocktails are also becoming part of the community's fabric.

— BASIL—AND? —

The cucumber and grapefruit shine in this fresh and clean gin cocktail with the Cuban—inspired name. A FINKA modern classic.

GLASSWARE: Rocks glass

GARNISH: Basil leaf

- 2 oz. Fifty Pounds Gin
- ¾ oz. fresh lemon juice
- ¾ oz. fresh cucumber juice
- ¾ oz. grapefruit syrup
- Dash of Bittermens Boston Bittahs
- 3 basil leaves

1. Combine all of the ingredients in a cocktail shaker filled with ice and shake vigorously.

2. Double-strain over a king cube* into a rocks glass and garnish with basil leaf.

FOR GRAPEFRUIT SYRUP: In a saucepan, combine a 2:1 ratio of simple syrup (see page 43) to fresh grapefruit juice; add a pinch of salt and a handful of rosemary. Bring to a boil and then remove from heat. Strain, cool for 8 hours, label, and store.

Available at Mixology Ice.

MOVERS & SHAKERS:

Eileen Andrade took a risk in opening FINKA Table and Tap, a progressive Cuban– and Asian–inspired restaurant in western Miami. The risk paid off, and the award–winning chef has introduced inventive cocktails to that neighborhood, igniting a movement.

— SAGED BY THE BELL —

FINKA TABLE AND TAP

Another FINKA classic. The floral, tangy hibiscus and garden–picked sage are highlighted by the agave in the tequila.

GLASSWARE: Rocks glass

GARNISH: Sage leaf

- 2 oz. Hornitos Plata Tequila
- ¾ oz. fresh lime juice
- 1 oz. spicy hibiscus syrup
- 3 to 4 sage leaves
- 2 dashes of Fee Brothers Peach Bitters

1. Combine all of the ingredients in a cocktail shaker filled with ice and shake vigorously.

2. Double–strain over a king cube into a rocks glass and garnish with a sage leaf.

FOR SPICY HIBISCUS SYRUP: In a saucepan, combine a 2:1 sugar–to–water ratio and add 1 cup of dehydrated local hibiscus and ají limo pepper (use 1 pepper per quart of water). Bring to a boil, remove from heat, and cool for 8 hours. Strain, label, and store.

LITTLE

HAVANA

Lying immediately west of Downtown Miami, Little Havana became home for many Cuban immigrants in the 1960s. Their mark on the area is evident on every street corner, from the restaurants and bars to the cigar shops and art galleries. In this area of Miami, Spanish is the predominant language.

— MOJITO —

BALL & CHAIN

While Mojitos are everywhere in Miami, a good one is hard to come by. With Little Havana as the backdrop, Ball & Chain makes one of the city's best.

GLASSWARE: Highball glass

GARNISH: Mint sprig

- ½ oz. lime juice
- 5 to 7 mint leaves
- ¾ oz. simple syrup (see page 43)
- 1½ oz. Bacardi Superior
- Soda water, to top

1. Place the lime juice and mint in a highball glass and gently muddle.

2. Add the simple syrup and rum.

3. Fill the glass with crushed ice and give the drink a good stir, making sure to combine all ingredients.

4. Add more crushed ice, top with soda water, and garnish with a mint sprig.

MOVERS & SHAKERS:

Zack Bush is one of the co-owners of Little Havana's favorite Cuban-inspired bar, Ball & Chain. With a delicious food menu and cocktails that articulate what's special in the area, it's no wonder Ball & Chain has become a favorite spot for Mojitos, Daiquiris, and Cuba Libres.

— CALLE OCHO OLD FASHIONED —

BALL & CHAIN

Miami is a rum city. So this Old Fashioned is made with rum. The tobacco-infused bitters will make you want to enjoy this drink with a cigar.

GLASSWARE: Rocks glass
GARNISH: Dry tobacco leaf

- **2 oz. Bacardi Ocho**
- **¼ oz. demerara syrup (see page 136)**

- **3 dashes of tobacco–infused bitters**

1. Place all of the ingredients in a mixing glass filled with ice and gently stir until chilled, about 8 seconds.

2. Strain over ice in a rocks glass and garnish with a dry tobacco leaf.

FOR TOBACCO–INFUSED BITTERS: Steep a small amount of tobacco leaves (1 or 2) in a 6.7 oz bottle of Angostura Bitters for 3 to 5 hours. Strain and store.

— LA CHANCLETA —

CAFÉ LA TROVA

Maestro Julio Cabrera brings his cantinero style to Little Havana with this simple yet tasty cocktail, which is served in a clay vessel that is *delivered* on a chancleta (flip-flop).

GLASSWARE: Clay vessel

GARNISH: Lime wheel

- 1 ½ oz. Avuá Cachaça Amburana
- ¾ oz. ginger-honey syrup
- ¾ oz. fresh lime juice

1. Combine all ingredients in a cocktail shaker filled with ice and shake vigorously.

2. Strain over ice into a clay vessel and garnish with a lime wheel.

FOR GINGER-HONEY SYRUP: In a saucepan, combine 2½ cups local honey, 1¼ cups water, and 1 big piece of finely chopped fresh ginger. Bring to a boil, then let cool. Strain, label, and store.

MOVERS & SHAKERS:

Julio Cabrera is considered one of the best cantineros to come out of Cuba. This former National Most Imaginative Bartender Winner once graced the cover of *GQ* and has become a go-to for anything Cuban. His bar, Café La Trova, brings Cuba to Miami's backyard with music, cigars, and Cuban-inspired cocktails made by the man himself.

— EL GUAYABERO —

CAFÉ LA TROVA

Combining guava, a Miami favorite, with citrus and tequila never tasted so good. Julio Cabrera creates a spicy syrup that is a perfect pairing with the timbita garnish.

GLASSWARE: Tall glass
GARNISH: Timbita (guava paste and fresh white cheese)*
speared on a cocktail umbrella

- **2 oz. Casa Noble Crystal Tequila**
- **¾ oz. guava marmalade****
- **¾ oz. cayenne-agave syrup**
- **¾ oz. fresh lime juice**

1. Combine all ingredients in a cocktail shaker filled with ice and shake vigorously.

2. Strain into glass over ice and garnish with timbita speared on cocktail umbrella.

FOR CAYENNE-AGAVE SYRUP: In a quart container, combine 2 cups agave nectar, 1 cup hot water, and 1 teaspoon of cayenne pepper. Shake until all ingredients are combined.

The guava paste and cheese are available in supermarkets or online; for the cheese, look for queso blanco, or other unaged cow's milk cheese.

**Available in supermarkets or online.*

— LA TROVA OLD FASHIONED —

CAFÉ LA TROVA

This rum Old Fashioned marries the flavors of rum and coffee. The chocolate bitters add a bit of decadence to this Miami version of a classic.

GLASSWARE: Rocks glass
GARNISH: Strip of orange peel and grated coffee bean

- 2 oz. Bacardi Ocho
- ⅓ oz. cafecito syrup

- 4 dashes of Scrappy's Chocolate Bitters

1. Add all ingredients to a mixing glass filled with ice and stir until chilled.

2. Strain over a large cube of ice in a rocks glass and garnish with an orange peel and grated coffee bean.

FOR CAFECITO SYRUP: In a bowl, combine 2 cups of demerera sugar, 1 cup hot water, and 1½ oz. espresso and mix until sugar is well dissolved. Let cool, label, and store.

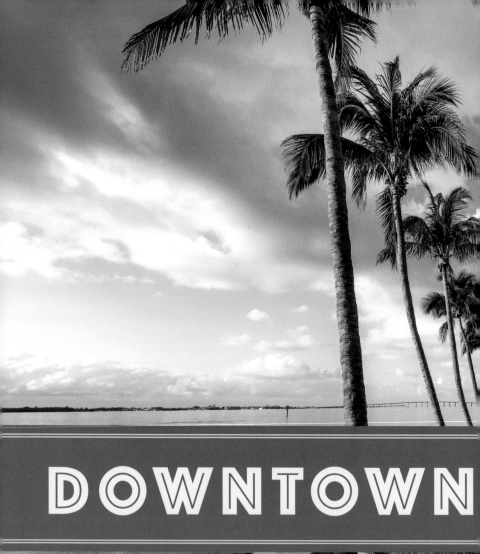

DOWNTOWN

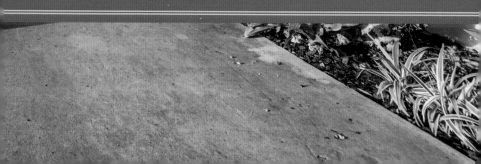

& BRICKELL

Downtown and Brickell were home to some of the Magic City's earliest settlers. The area continues to grow at a rapid pace with new bars and restaurants opening every month amid the many historical buildings. All of a sudden, great cocktails can be found blocks from Biscayne Bay.

MOVERS & SHAKERS:

You've probably had a cocktail in one of his establishments and didn't know Dan Binkiewicz was behind it. His vision of serving up great hospitality and cocktails has stood the test of time and helped bring high–volume bars and great cocktails together. Blackbird Ordinary, The Bar, Purdy Lounge, and Sweet Liberty are just a few of the legendary spots he's had a hand in.

— BLACKBIRD —

BLACKBIRD ORDINARY

Blackbird Ordinary is in the heart of downtown Brickell and has been serving up consistently great cocktails for years. The Blackbird is one of its signatures and is perfect to sip on their outdoor patio. The sweet tea vodka and blackberry are perfect together.

GLASSWARE: Pint glass
GARNISH: Blackberry and a mint sprig

- 2 oz. sweet tea vodka
- ½ oz. blackberry puree
- ¾ oz. fresh lemon juice
- ¾ oz. simple syrup (see page 43)

1. Place all of the ingredients in a cocktail shaker filled with ice.

2. Shake and then strain into a pint glass.

3. Add pebble ice.*

4. Garnish with a blackberry and a mint sprig.

If pebble ice isn't available, use crushed ice.

— THE WOODPECKER —

BLACKBIRD ORDINARY

Who says whiskey isn't a summer spirit? Ginger and whiskey go together like sunshine and the beach. This simple combination crafted in a mason jar is perfect for sitting poolside with friends.

GLASSWARE: Mason jar

GARNISH: Candied ginger*

- 2 oz. Woodford Reserve
- 1 oz. ginger syrup (see page 69)
- ¼ oz. fresh lime juice
- 3 dashes of aromatic bitters
- Soda water, to top

1. Place all of the ingredients in a mason jar filled with ice, except for the soda water.

2. Stir until blended.

3. Top with soda water and garnish with candied ginger.

Candied ginger is delicious on its own and can be found online or at your local supermarket.

MOVERS & SHAKERS:

Paul Cleary is one of Blackbird Ordinary's head bartenders and can be found there on any given day serving up great hospitality and seamless cocktails. Cleary has never been one to join cocktail competitions or seek out the spotlight, but he cares about his craft and is one of the best bartenders in Miami.

— PEONY —

EAST, MIAMI

This vodka cocktail with a rum attitude combines the best of both worlds and adds island accents of pineapple and coconut. Delicious.

GLASSWARE: Highball glass

GARNISH: Any edible flower and a lime wheel

- 1½ oz. Absolut Elyx
- 2 oz. pineapple juice
- 2 oz. coconut syrup
- ⅛ oz. fresh lime juice
- 8 mint leaves
- Ron Zacapa rum, to float

1. Place all of the ingredients in a cocktail shaker filled with ice, except the rum, and shake until chilled.

2. Strain over ice into a highball glass and float the rum on top.

3. Garnish with an edible flower and a lime wheel.

— SACRED LOTUS —

Tamarind adds a tangy note of citrus to the vodka and is balanced by the St–Germain. Topped off with prosecco and fruit, you get East's version of a sangria.

GLASSWARE: Wine glass

GARNISH: Cucumber slice, mixed berries, a lemon wheel, and an orange slice

- 1 oz. tamarind–infused Belvedere Vodka
- 1 oz. St–Germain
- Prosecco, to top

1. Place the vodka and St–Germain in a wine glass, add ice, and top with the Prosecco.

2. Garnish with a cucumber slice, mixed berries, a lemon wheel, and an orange slice.

FOR THE TAMARIND-INFUSED VODKA: Place ⅓ cup peeled and seeded tamarind in a mason jar filled with vodka and store in a cool, dark place for 1 week, while shaking daily.

— PINEAPPLE EXPRESS —

KOMODO

Asimple yet tasty take on a margarita that is finished off with mezcal mist and fresh pineapple juice for the perfect amount of froth.

GLASSWARE: Rocks glass
GARNISH: Spiced salt* and a pineapple ring

- 2 oz. Casamigos Tequila
- 1 oz. Thai chili agave
- 1 oz. fresh lime juice
- 2 oz. pineapple juice
- Mezcal mist, to top

1. Combine all of the ingredients, except for the mezcal mist, in a cocktail shaker filled with ice and shake until cold.

2. Double-strain over ice into a rocks glass.

3. Mist mezcal over cocktail and garnish with spiced salt and a pineapple ring.

FOR THAI CHILI AGAVE: Add ½ lb. Thai chilis to ½ gallon of water and bring to a boil. Add ½ gallon of agave nectar and simmer for 1 hour. Let cool, strain, label, and store.

Find a spiced salt that suits your palate online or at a specialty market.

— SEASONAL G&T —

Lost Boy Dry Goods doubles as a denim boutique during the day and serves badass cocktails when the sun begins to fall.

GLASSWARE: Goblet

GARNISH: Lemon expression (discard), dehydrated candied lemon wheel, and a rosemary tip

- 1½ oz. Portobello Road Gin
- ¼ oz. Mancino Secco Vermouth
- East Imperial Grapefruit Tonic, to top

1. Place the gin and vermouth in a goblet and top with the tonic. Express the lemon peel over the cocktail and discard.

2. Garnish with the dehydrated candied lemon wheel and a rosemary tip.

FOR DEHYDRATED CANDIED LEMON WHEEL: Preheat oven to 275°F. Cut 4 lemons into wheels and arrange on a parchment-lined baking sheet. Sprinkle ½ cup sugar over lemon wheels. Bake for 40 to 50 minutes, until lemons look like candy. Let cool and carefully peel off parchment paper.

— LOST BOY PENICILLIN —

LOST BOY DRY GOODS

S am Ross created the original Penicillin cocktail. This tribute to him does not stray from the original recipe but instead uses local honey—a perfect Miami whisky cocktail.

GLASSWARE: Rocks glass

GARNISH: Candied ginger

- **Dash of Laprhroaig, to wash**
- **2 oz. The Glenlivet Founder's Reserve**
- **¾ oz. fresh lemon juice**
- **¾ oz. orange blossom honey– ginger syrup**

1. Add a dash of Laphroaig to a rocks glass and coat the inside of the glass.

2. Combine all of the remaining ingredients in a cocktail shaker with ice, shake vigorously, and strain over ice into the rocks glass.

3. Garnish with candied ginger.

FOR ORANGE BLOSSOM HONEY-GINGER SYRUP: First, make orange blossom honey syrup by adding 1 cup orange blossom honey to 1 cup water and bringing to a boil in a saucepan; then let cool. Then combine 2 parts fresh ginger juice to 1 part orange blossom honey syrup.

— RASPBERRY BERET —

MAMA TRIED

This delicious ode to Prince allows you to select your spirit of choice. Want to use gin? It works! Rum? That too. Just follow the recipe and it'll be delicious.

GLASSWARE: Sling glass
GARNISH: Mint sprig, raspberries, and a pink peppercorn

- 1½ oz. Fords Gin
- ¾ oz. fresh lemon juice
- ¾ oz. simple syrup (see page 43)
- ½ oz. Cocchi Rosa
- 4 raspberries
- Prosecco, to top

1. Place all of the ingredients in a cocktail shaker filled with ice, except for the Prosecco, and shake until chilled.

2. Strain over crushed ice in a Sling glass, then add the Prosecco and more crushed ice.

3. Garnish with a mint sprig, 4 raspberries, and a pink peppercorn.

— MAMA'S PORN STAR MARTINI —

MAMA TRIED

A Miami spin on this homage to Douglas Ankrah, creator of the Porn Star Martini.

GLASSWARE: Coupe and a champagne flute
GARNISH: Filthy Cherry*

- **2 oz. Absolut Vanilla**
- **¾ oz. passion fruit puree**
- **¾ oz. fresh pineapple juice**
- **¾ oz. Licor 43**
- **Pinch of Maldon sea salt**
- **Sidecar of sparkling wine**

1. Combine all of the ingredients in a cocktail shaker filled with ice, except for the sparkling wine, shake until chilled, and strain into a coupe.

2. Fill a champagne flute halfway with the sparkling wine and garnish with a Filthy Cherry.

Filthy Foods makes some of best cocktail garnishes, which are widely available in specialty stores and online.

— LA DIOSA —

Taking cues from the margarita, the egg white texture and chili heat give this riff a character of its own.

GLASSWARE: Coupe
GARNISH: Micro flowers and house Tajin

- 1½ oz. tequila
- ¾ oz. triple sec
- ½ oz. fresh lime juice
- 1 tablespoon pineapple marmalade
- ½ spoonful of dried chili
- Small bunch of cilantro
- 1 egg white

1. Place all of the ingredients in a cocktail shaker filled with ice, except for the egg white, and shake until chilled. Strain, discard ice, return cocktail ingredients to shaker, add egg white, and shake.

2. Strain into a coupe and garnish with micro flowers and house Tajin.

FOR PINEAPPLE MARMALADE: In a saucepan, combine 4 peeled, cored, and cubed pineapples; 8 cinnamon sticks; ¼ cup vanilla extract; 4 orange peels; 2 seeded Guajillo chilies; 1 cup sweet vermouth; 1 cup Lillet Blanc; and 4 cups sugar. Simmer for 5 hours until liquid is reduced by at least half. Remove cinnamon sticks and chilies and then puree remaining mixture. Label, date, and refrigerate.

FOR HOUSE TAJIN: Blend 1 cup mesquite seasoning, 1 cup smoky paprika, and ½ cup kosher salt in a container; add zest of 2 grapefruits. Label, date, and store.

— THE MADE AND THE BORN —

MO BAR + LOUNGE AT THE MANDARIN ORIENTAL

Styled much like an Old Fashioned, this cocktail brings out the smooth and complex notes of the gin's botanicals, delivering your palate a surprising twist.

GLASSWARE: Rocks glass

GARNISH: Strips of lemon and lime peel and grated nutmeg

- 2 oz. blended gin
- ½ oz. bourbon syrup
- 2 dashes of Peychaud's Bitters
- 2 dashes of Angostura Bitters

1. Combine all of the ingredients in a mixing glass filled with ice and stir until chilled.

2. Strain over an ice cube in a rocks glass and garnish with strips of lemon and lime peel and grated nutmeg.

FOR BLENDED GIN: Combine ¾ Tanqueray with ¼ St. George Terroir.

FOR BOURBON SYRUP: Place a saucepan over low heat and combine 2 parts sugar, 1 part water, and 1 part bourbon. Simmer, while stirring, until sugar is dissolved.

SURFSIDE

When tire tycoon Harvey Firestone and notable Miamians Carl Fisher and Irving Collins came up with the idea for The Surf Club, little could they have known that the club, which opened in 1930, would inspire the name for this neighborhood, just a stone's throw away from Miami Beach. Today, Le Sirenuse inhabits the club's original building, and its cocktails evoke the days when the likes of Frank Sinatra, Dean Martin, and Elizabeth Taylor were frequent guests.

— FIORI | FLOWERS —

Bergamot liqueur lends delicate citrus notes to this drink as the kiwi-and-basil shrub add fruit and acidity. The elderflower soda ties it all together while highlighting the floral jasmine tea.

GLASSWARE: Tulip glass
GARNISH: Edible Egyptian flower

- 1½ oz. jasmine tea–infused vodka
- ¾ oz. bergamot liqueur
- 1 oz. fresh lemon juice
- ¾ oz. kiwi–and–basil shrub
- 1 oz. elderflower soda, to top
- Flower essence,* to top

1. Combine all of the ingredients, except for the elderflower soda and the flower essence, in a cocktail shaker filled with ice and shake until chilled.

2. Strain over an ice sphere in a tulip glass and top with elderflower soda and flower essence.

3. Garnish with an edible Egyptian flower.

Le Sirenuse uses a house–made distillate essence of 3 flowers: roses, petunias, and geraniums (the main flowers of Positano on Italy's Amalfi Coast). A variety of flower essences are available online.

FOR JASMINE TEA-IN-FUSED VODKA: Place 10 jasmine tea bags in 1 liter of vodka; let steep for 12 hours.

FOR KIWI-AND-BASIL SHRUB: Wash and quarter 5½ pounds kiwi (with the skin). In pan, combine kiwi with 3½ cups sugar; cover and let the fruit and sugar macerate overnight. Combine 3½ oz. basil leaves, 1½ cups apple cider vinegar, and 3 cups filtered water and cover overnight. Next day, strain the kiwi juice into a small bowl. Strain infused vinegar mixture. Combine strained kiwi mixture with the strained infused vinegar and whisk well to incorporate any undissolved sugar. Pour mixture into a mason jar, cap it, shake it, and place it in refrigerator for 1 week.

— TERRA I SOIL —

LE SIRENUSE

The nuttiness from the hazelnut combined with the Amaro, dates, and honey syrup create a perfect balance in both the taste and smell. The nutty tonalities lend themselves to herbaceous notes, which finish with the truffle salt on the palate.

GLASSWARE: Rocks glass

- 2 oz. hazelnut–infused bourbon
- ¼ oz. Bonollo Amaro Of
- ¼ oz. date–and–honey syrup
- 3 dashes of pimento bitters
- 2 dashes of truffle salt

1. Combine all of the ingredients in a mixing glass filled with ice and stir until chilled.

2. Strain over a large ice cube in a rocks glass.

DESIGN

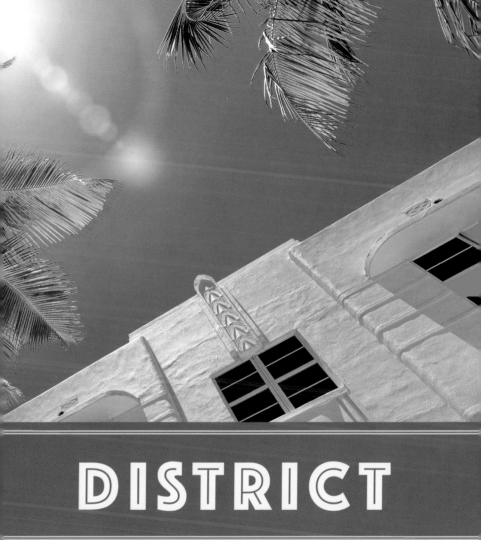

DISTRICT

The Design District is famous for art galleries, design houses, and fashion spaces. The neighborhood retains its cool Miami charm with bars and restaurants nestled between some of the world's greatest luxury brands.

— ENFUEGO —

This Design District spot has become legendary for its contemporary bistro cuisine, gorgeous bar program, and stunningly seamless hospitality. This drink gets its name from the spicy serrano syrup, which goes swimmingly with the fresh watermelon juice and tequila.

GLASSWARE: Collins glass
GARNISH: Raw jalapeño slice

- **Basil-lime zest salt, for the rim**
- **2 oz. Milagro tequila**
- **1 oz. watermelon juice**
- **¾ oz. hibiscus-serrano syrup**
- **½ oz. fresh lime juice**

1. Wet the rim of a Collins glass and dip it into the basil-lime zest salt.

2. Combine the remaining ingredients in a cocktail shaker filled with ice and shake until chilled. Fill the glass with ice and strain the cocktail into it.

3. Garnish with a jalapeño slice.

FOR BASIL-LIME ZEST SALT RIM: Roast equal parts basil and lime zest in the oven at 350°F for 20 minutes. Blend in coffee grinder. Add equal amount of salt to lime zest-basil blend.

FOR HIBISCUS-SERRANO SYRUP: In a saucepan, combine 1 cup dry hibiscus, 5 serrano peppers (chopped), 2 quarts sugar, and 2 quarts water and bring to a boil. Simmer until liquid has reduced by a quarter.

— CABARETE —

MICHAEL'S GENUINE FOOD & DRINK

Punctuated by the fresh watermelon juice, St-Germain and Aperol are best friends in this light sipper, a brunch favorite at Michael's.

GLASSWARE: Wine glass

GARNISH: Strip of grapefruit peel

- 1½ oz. fresh watermelon juice
- ¾ oz. St-Germain
- ¾ oz. Aperol
- 2 dashes of orange bitters
- Prosecco, to top

Add all ingredients to a wine glass filled with ice and garnish with a strip of grapefruit peel.

ncorporated in 2000, the town of Miami Lakes is a world of its own. With bars and restaurants lining the streets, it's no wonder that local residents never leave. Everything you need is nestled in this area of less than 7 square miles, especially one particularly excellent bar serving up local beers and fresh cocktails.

— PAINKILLER —

THE BEND

The Painkiller is the signature cocktail of Pusser's Rum, and has Miami written all over it. At The Bend, it's one of the most popular drinks.

GLASSWARE: Pusser's Painkiller vessel or rocks glass
GARNISH: Grated nutmeg and an orange slice

- 2 oz. Pusser's Rum
- 1 oz. coconut cream
- 1 oz. orange juice
- 4 oz. pineapple juice

1. Combine all ingredients with ice in a blender and flash blend.*

2. Pour into glass over ice and garnish with fresh grated nutmeg and a slice of orange.

This technique is used to blend the drink in a standing mixer, creating a wonderful texture. Think of the old-style blenders, like the ones used for milkshakes. A standard blender will do the job as well. If no blender is on hand, shake ingredients with ice and do not strain before serving.

— MO'S MAI TAI —

THE BEND

A perfectly made Mai Tai is not easy to come by but The Bend nails it. With the blend of rum and rhum, this version transports you to paradise.

GLASSWARE: Rocks glass
GARNISH: Spent lime shell and mint sprig

- 1½ oz. Appleton Estate Signature Rum
- ½ oz. La Favorite Rhum Agricole Blanc
- ¼ oz. simple syrup (see page 43)
- ¼ oz. Giffard Orgeat Syrup
- ½ oz. dry curaçao

1. Combine all ingredients in a cocktail shaker filled with ice and shake vigorously.

2. Strain over ice in a rocks glass and garnish with a spent lime shell and a mint sprig.

MIAMI'S BEST

OF THE BEST

Miami is known for many different foods, cocktails, dive bars, and everything in between. The blend of different cultures from around the world gives the Magic City its character and personality. Miami is one of those wonderful places where you can find 10 different types of food or drink from places all over the world—all within 5 minutes of each other. This list should serve only as an introductory guide, as there are many other establishments that can compete for the title of best of the best. Like the famous quote credited to Ernest Hemingway, "My mojito in La Bodeguita, my daiquiri in El Floridita," I too cannot pinpoint one place that's my favorite all the time. You should approach this list the same way.

FRITA CUBANA

Fritas are a staple in Miami culinary culture and are a fast, delicious Cuban-style burger made for a night on the town. With origins dating back to 1930s Cuban street food, the crisp crust of the Cuban roll, paprika and cumin seasoning, and shoestring fried potato topping set this a burger apart. The frita has won its way into the hearts of Miami's locals over the years. According to Burger Beast, the frita was brought over from Cuba in 1961 when Dagoberto Estevil opened in Little Havana.

PLACES TO GO: El Rey de las Fritas • Ariete • La Palma • Palomilla Grill • Amelia's 1931 • Cuban Guys • Fritas Domino La Original • El Mago de las Fritas

MOJITOS

Did Miami invent the Mojito? No, but we sure know how to make a tasty, refreshing one. The key is balance: not too sweet, not too sour, and make sure to let the rum shine while the subtle hints of mint cool you off.

PLACES TO GO: Mango's Tropical Cafe • Ball & Chain • Havana 1957 • Tap Tap • Esquina De La Fama • Cubaocho Museum and Performing Arts Center • La Casa de la Trova • The Regent Cocktail Club • SUGARCANE Raw Bar Grill

MARGARITAS

We love a tasty, balanced Margarita with 100 percent agave tequila. Perfect for Miami's hot and humid summers.

PLACES TO GO: Sweet Liberty • Bodega Taqueria y Tequila • Taquiza • The Bazaar by José Andrés • Rocco's Tacos & Tequila Bar • Tacology • Coyo Taco • Cantina La Veinte • TacoCraft

BURGERS

It's always a good time for a BBQ in Miami, so why not have a best burgers list? It's always hard to argue with the Miami local, Burger Beast, where the proprietor has dedicated his life to finding the best burgers around, but here are our personal favorites.

PLACES TO GO: Ariete • Pincho Factory • Shake Shack • The Local • LoKal • Hole in the Wall • Proper Sausages • Bryson's Irish Pub • Cheeseburger Baby • Bocas Grill • Hillstone

CAFECITOS

Have you tried Miami's version of an energy drink? Roll up to one of Miami's "ventanitas" (small takeout windows) for a midday pick-me-up. It's a ritual that is shared by many Miamians, and is celebrated every day at 3:05 p.m.

PLACES TO GO: El Exquisito • La Carreta • Sergio's Restaurant • Vicky Bakery • Versailles Cuban Bakery • Polo Norte • Islas Canarias Bakery

CUBAN FOOD

This is a competitive category in a city that loves its Cuban food. Here, we are looking for a great, inexpensive, traditional Cuban meal.

PLACES TO GO: Islas Canarias Bakery • Sergio's Cuban Café • Vicky Bakery • Palomilla Grill • Polo Norte • Morro Castle • Las Palmas • Versailles Cuban Bakery • La Carreta • El Exquisito • El Palacio de los Jugos

COLOMBIAN FOOD

Colombian food is a staple in Miami that has become a popular late-night snack.

PLACES TO GO: La Estacion Cafe • El Patio 305 • Patacon Pisao • Rincón Antioqueño Restaurant • El Palacio de los Frijoles • Pueblito Viejo • Los Arrieros • La Ventana Restaurant • Manantial Market Place • Sanpocho Restaurant

HOT DOGS

Hot dogs are one of America's favorite foods, and Miami does a great job of creating its own version.

PLACES TO GO: Sweet Dogs 305 • Los Verdes • Pincho Factory • Arbetter's Hot Dogs • Los Perros • Miami Smokers • La Moon Restaurant

BREWERIES

Our beer producers have been hard at work quenching the thirst of South Florida's locals with some of the tastiest beers around. You can expect to find tropical beers, locally sourced ingredients, and more. Some even make cocktails with their own beer!

PLACES TO GO: Veza Sur Brewing Co. • Lincoln's Beard Brewing Co. • Bousa Brewing • M.I.A. Beer Company • The Tank Brewing Co. • J. Wakefield Brewing • Wynwood Brewing Company • Biscayne Bay Brewing Company • Concrete Beach Brewery • Unbranded Brewing Co.

ICE CREAM AND GELATO

It's Miami, the average temperature in the summer months is 85°F with an average humidity of over 70 percent. It's hot, it's humid, and the only answer is ice cream. I love these spots for their local ingredients, Cuban flair, and boozy, frozen goodness.

PLACES TO GO: Azucar Ice Cream Company • Cream Parlor • Whip'n Dip Ice Cream Shop • AUBI & RAMSA • Bianco Gelato • Wynwood Parlor • The Frieze Ice Cream Factory • Sweet Melody Ice Cream • Dasher & Crank • Miami Coppelia Ice Cream

DOUGHNUTS

Miami has been enamored with doughnuts for a long time, and the fever is now at an all-time high. With plenty of doughnut shops opening their doors and featuring some crazy local flavors—as well as some that are not so local—there are plenty to choose from.

PLACES TO GO: Honeybee Doughnuts • The Salty Donut • Mojo Donuts & Fried Chicken • Velvet Creme Doughnuts & Coffee • Happy Place Donuts • Donutty

TACOS

Tacos are probably one of my favorite things right now. From carnitas to fish and veggie, they're all covered here.

PLACES TO GO: Taquiza • Cantina La Veinte • Coyo Taco • TacoCraft • Jacalito Taqueria Mexicana • Huahua's Taqueria • El Taquito • Sandbar Sports Grill • Plomo Tequila & Taco Bar • Tacos El Carnal

LIQUOR STORES

It's not always easy finding ingredients around Miami, and wine and spirits are no different. Liquor store selections vary around Miami, but a few choice locations have everything you need to make that special cocktail.

PLACES TO GO: Sunset Corners • Vintage Liquor • Crown Wine & Spirits • Big Game Liquors • Jensen's Liquor

CIGAR SHOPS

How are you going to sip on your rum Old Fashioned while playing dominos without a damn good cigar? Your search starts here.

PLACES TO GO: Stogie's Fine Cigars • Neptune Cigars • Little Havana Cigar Factory • Cuban Crafters • Padrón Cigars • Casa De Montecristo by Prime Cigar & Whiskey Bar • Art District Cigars • Gables Cigars • Coco Cigars • Aficionados Brickell

INDEX

Cocktail recipes included in the book are in italics.

ABOUT THE AUTHOR

Gabriel Fernando Urrutia enjoys educating bartenders and consumers about Bacardi's dynamic Single Malts portfolio. Urrutia brings over 14 years of hospitality experience to his role and considers it a privilege to work with Bacardi USA's single malt brands. In his previous roles, he has conducted more than 150 training sessions for bartenders, while drawing on his creativity and knowledge to develop over 75 fresh and exciting cocktail menus. In 2009, he was nominated and shortlisted for "Young Achiever of The Year" at the London International Wine Fair; he was the only nominee from the United States. Urrutia was also a finalist for St-Germain's Can-Can competition in 2011 and winner of the National DeKuyper Challenge in 2016.

—ABOUT CIDER MILL PRESS BOOK PUBLISHERS—

Good ideas ripen with time. From seed to harvest, Cider Mill Press
brings fine reading, information, and entertainment together between
the covers of its creatively crafted books. Our Cider Mill bears fruit
twice a year, publishing a new crop of titles each spring and fall.

"Where Good Books Are Ready for Press"

Visit us on the web at
www.cidermillpress.com

or write to us at
PO Box 454
12 Spring St.
Kennebunkport, Maine 04046